CAREGIVERS WORK:

A SIX STEP GUIDE TO BALANCING

WORK AND FAMILY

CAREGIVERS WORK:

A SIX STEP GUIDE TO BALANCING WORK AND FAMILY

ELDER CARE EDITION

JOHN PAUL MAROSY

Caregivers Work

CaregiversWork LLC

Denver, CO

© Copyright 2019.

Originally published as *Elder Care: A Six Step Guide to Balancing Work and Family* (2002).

Illustrations by Maura Zimmer.

Book design by Sarah Beaudin.

Printed in the United States of America.

ISBN: 978-0-9716462-2-3

www.caregiverswork.com

This book is dedicated to hospice care professionals and volunteers everywhere.

CONTENTS

ACKNOWLEDGMENTS

Many thanks to the following people who provided insights, suggestions,
and advice for this guide:

Sarah Alan, Esq.

Jack Beauregard

Hannah Benoit

Mary Brintnall-Peterson, Ph.D.

Jack Curley

Peg Cushman

Elaine Delaney-Winn

Michelle DeMeritt

Mary Jane Dixon

Brian Duke

Rev. Dr. Gregory Edwards

Susan Donahue Erler

Guillermo Gonzalez

Eboni Green, Ph.D., RN

Terrence Green

Rick Greene

Cliff Hakim

Joanne Handy

Donna Huron

Linda Jones

Lawrence Kron, Ph.D.

Robert Lavelle

Arlene Lowney

Martin Marosy

Thomas Pierre Marosy

Suzanne Geffen Mintz

Robert O'Toole

Lori Ross

Wendy Salguero

Mark Sciegaj, Ph.D.

Vicki Schmall, Ph.D.

Connie Siskowski, Ph.D.

Ronnette Virginia Smith

Bern Terry

Hillary Turkewitz

Karla Vineyard

Dianne Weber

Donna Wagner, Ph.D.

Neal Winston, Esq.

ACKNOWLEDGEMENTS

PREFACE

When my father, Michael "Jack" Marosy informed our family that he had been diagnosed with prostate cancel, I had been working as an administrator in home care and elder care for the previous fifteen years.

I had worked as an administrator in home care and elder care for fifteen years prior to his announcement. Yet, nothing in my professional experience had prepared me for the emotional roller coaster ride of caregiving for my dad. Over the next two years, I learned firsthand what it's like to try to balance work responsibilities with arranging the right care as Jack's condition declined. It wasn't easy. Ultimately, my family members and I succeeded. We helped Jack fulfill his final wish: to die at home in comfort. It required a united effort that included a wonderful hospice care team—a doctor, nurse, social worker, home health aide and volunteers.

Since publication of the first edition, titled *Elder Care: A Six Step Guide to Balancing Work and Family,* the number of U.S. workers grappling with caregiving has increased dramatically. And the Census Bureau has announced that, with the aging of the baby boomers, older people will soon outnumber children for the first time in U.S. history. So, if you're dealing with caregiving/work balance issues, you've got lots of company! This new edition contains updated information on the expanding resources available to help you find balance.

As this book's title implies, caregiving is a job. The work you perform as a caregiver has value to you, your family, and your community. Our society has yet to fully recognize that value. In fact, the U.S. is the only industrialized nation that does not assure paid family leave for all its citizens involved in caregiving. We have a long way to go.

That being said, you can succeed in balancing caregiving and work. This book gives you what I lacked: a road map and a set of tools for the caregiving journey. So, let's get started!

John Paul Marosy

PART I

PERSPECTIVES AND PRINCIPLES

About This Guide—and Family Caregiving

    " Anyone can become a caregiver at
a moment's notice. All it takes is a stroke,
an accident, or a debilitating illness—
and someone you love. **"**
—Suzanne Geffen Mintz, Founder
Caregiver Action Network

The purpose of this guide is to provide insight and guidance for the employee or business owner who is—or soon will be—arranging care for an older parent or loved one who is sick or disabled.

Juggling responsibilities for raising your family, performing your job, and caring for your older relative can be stressful. However, you can also reap rewards from the caregiving experience. For some, arranging care for an older relative in declining health can provide an opportunity to heal relationships and to "give back" to an older person who may have given much to you earlier in life. Others may find themselves being drawn into supportive or caregiving situations that have involved a painful history or in which they have tried to distance themselves to maintain their own health or well-being.

This guide can help you with the caregiving/work balancing act. It starts with definitions of balance and effective caregiving and sets out four principles that can help make the caregiving experience a positive one. Then, it describes a six-step process that you can use to develop your own unique plan to find and maintain balance.

The last section, *Elder Care Resources from A-Z*, includes phone numbers and websites where you can obtain help and guidance.

The goals for this guide are to help you

- make the best choices you can to assure the well-being of your older loved one
- maintain your own good health
- remain productive at your job

PREPARING FOR THE JOURNEY: YOU ARE NOT ALONE!

If you find yourself involved in caregiving: take heart! You are not alone. In fact, one in four households includes a family caregiver—and most caregivers also work outside the home.

Most people in their sixties and seventies live active, vibrant lives. However, persons over age 85—the fastest growing age group—are more likely than others to need help with everyday tasks like shopping, transportation, dressing, and bathing. Most of that help is provided by family members, not by agencies, assisted living residences, or nursing homes. Family caregivers provide 80% of all home care in the United States.

Employers are feeling the impact of the increasing number of employees dealing with caregiving. According to the 2016 National Study of Employers by the Society for Human Resource Management (SHRM), 78% of employers offer an elder care resource and referral benefit (see page 39), and 38% offer a Dependent Care Assistance Program benefit (see page 36) which allows the employee to pay for elder care-related expenses with pre-tax dollars.

A 2015 report by the Family Caregiving Alliance (FCA) and AARP shows that more than 1 in 6 Americans working full-time or part-time are assisting with the care of an elderly or disabled family member, relative, or friend. Providing this assistance significantly affects one's work life. About a quarter of working caregivers are middle-aged and 13% are aged between 18 and 29.

IMPACT ON WORKING CAREGIVERS

According to FCA and AARP, 70% of working caregivers suffer work-related difficulties due to their dual roles. About half of all caregivers feel they have no choice about taking on caregiving responsibilities.

Nearly 70% of working caregivers caring for a family member or friend report having to rearrange their work schedule, decrease their hours, or take an unpaid leave in order to meet their caregiving responsibilities.

Six of ten caregivers experience at least one change in their employment due to caregiving such as cutting back work hours, taking a leave of absence, or receiving a warning about performance/attendance. About 6% give up working entirely—a result that this workbook intends to help you avoid.

Women may suffer a particularly high level of economic hardship due to caregiving. They are more likely than men to make alternate work arrangements: taking a less demanding job, giving up work entirely and losing job-related benefits.

IMPACT ON EMPLOYERS

You may wish to share with your employer these facts from the report by FCA and AARP:

Only half of working caregivers report that their work supervisor is aware of their caregiving responsibilities.

About half of all employers offer flexible work hours/paid sick days. One-third of employers offer paid family leave, and about one-quarter offer employee assistance programs or allow telecommuting.

One out of four working caregivers feel that caring for an aging family member, relative, or friend has an impact on their work performance and keeps them from working more hours.

The cost of caregiving in terms of lost productivity to U.S. businesses is $17.1 to $33 billion annually. These costs include absenteeism ($5.1 billion), shifts from full-time to part-time work ($4.8 billion), replacing employees ($6.6 billion), and workday adjustments ($6.3 billion). Many of these losses can be prevented by providing working caregivers with timely information, job schedule flexibility, and emotional support.

Employed caregivers cost their employers an estimated 8%—an additional $13.4 billion per year—more in health care costs than employees without caregiving responsibilities. Encouraging preventive health measures among caregivers can help with insurance costs.

EMPLOYER BEST PRACTICES

The FCA/AARP report lists these best practices. Which are offered by your employer?

1. Adopt a policy valuing caregiver employees based on job performance rather than holding them to outdated assumptions that they are not committed to their jobs.

2. Allow workplace flexibility, which provides alternate work arrangements: flex-time, compressed workweeks (i.e., working 10-hour days), part-time or working fewer hours for part of the year, and telecommuting.

3. For hourly employees on more strict schedules, do away with no-fault absenteeism policies that provide termination based on number of tardies or absences no matter the reason.

4. Provide education and training to supervisors and managers about having caregivers on the job and what constitutes caregiver discrimination.

5. Offer elder care support, resources, and referral services to caregiver employees. By doing so, employers benefit from better worker retention, improved productivity, lower stress, and improved morale and physical health among workers.

6. Implement recruitment practices for persons with caregiving responsibilities to target the hiring of skilled caregiver individuals who are looking to reenter the job market after caregiving.

> " The question is not how to get work and life in balance. It's about how to integrate the various threads that make you uniquely who you are; and especially about how to step back and see the fullness of the story unfolding in your life. "
>
> —Nan Langowitz

PERSONAL BALANCE

What do we mean by personal balance? How do we know when we have achieved it?

TOWARD DYNAMIC BALANCE

One notion of balance involves achieving a fixed, mechanical state of equilibrium between two opposites (e.g., work and family) at a single point in time. This idea of balance calls to mind the image of a mechanical scale like the one shown in Figure One. If you add too much weight to the left (work) side of the scale, then that side will tilt sharply downward, throwing off the balance with the right (family) side—and vice versa. In this model, the person is caught in the middle, like the fulcrum of the scale, at the center of a near-impossible balancing act, constantly struggling to adjust an out-of-kilter situation.

FIGURE ONE: THE SCALE REPRESENTS THE OLD, MECHANICAL NOTION OF BALANCE.

FIGURE TWO: THE WAVE PATTERN REPRESENTS A NEW, DYNAMIC NOTION OF BALANCE.

Scientific research tells us that balance is a basic characteristic of the universe, a dynamic process involving constant change. In his book, *The Power of Balance*, Jack Beauregard points to the wave as a fundamental, universal image of balance, with its rising crest and descending trough repeating over and over. "The wave pattern," he writes, "is reflected everywhere—in the repeated transition from day to night; in numerous biological patterns in our own bodies such as the heart's constant contraction and expansion and our on-going experience of breathing in and breathing out; and in every other area of life." The image of a series of waves (Figure Two) represents dynamic balance.

We can think of our lives as moving and changing over time like an ocean wave with its crests and troughs. When we recognize that the stresses and challenges we face will change over time, varying in intensity, we can gain a perspective that allows for developing a sense of balance over time.

One key to achieving a personal sense of dynamic balance is to find our sense of centeredness—a timeless, unchanging feeling of calm and serenity. There are many ways to access the inner calm that is our natural state. Practices like mindfulness meditation and yoga, as well as various forms of prayer, exercise, and experiencing nature are among the paths taken by individuals to experience centeredness. Your approach to finding your own center may or may not involve some form of spiritual or religious practice. In his classic book, *The Relaxation Response*, Herbert Benson, M.D., cites scientific evidence that shows the positive physiological and psychological benefits of engaging in certain conscious activities (e.g., bringing one's awareness to one's breathing) in response to felt stress. His book describes specific mind-body techniques that can enable one to achieve, on a regular basis, one's own sense of centeredness and calm.

DYNAMIC BALANCE IN RELATION TO CAREGIVING/WORK

Taking responsibility for caring for an older person can feel like an impossible task—a hardship that will necessarily throw your life out of balance.

Making caregiving/work balance a possible task means moving toward a sense of personal balance. By making a commitment to yourself to seek your inner center—and following the principles and techniques described in the following pages—you can engage in effective caregiving and begin to experience a sense of personal, dynamic balance.

Feeling stressed right now? Visit this link for immediate instruction in mindfulness-based stress reduction http://bit.ly/2u9ZQ18, and see page 77 for more caregiver support resources.

&& There are only four kinds of people in this world:
Those who are caregivers.
Those who were caregivers.
Those who will be caregivers.
And those who will need the help of a caregiver. **,,**

—Former First Lady Rosalynn Carter

EFFECTIVE CAREGIVING

WHO IS A FAMILY CAREGIVER? AND WHAT IS EFFECTIVE CAREGIVING?

If you have a deep personal relationship with a person who is chronically ill or disabled and your own life has been impacted by his or her condition, you are a family caregiver. You don't have to live in the same house—or the same state or country—as the person for whom you care. In fact, this guide includes a section devoted to the needs of long-distance caregivers. (p. 67)

Caregiving is a job. The successful performance of the job of caregiving requires the right attitude, the right skills, and the right information for your situation.

To perform well in the work place, you need to be organized, alert and healthy. The same applies to caregiving.

Effective caregiving means:

- Taking care of your own health and well-being as you help the older person in your life.
- Achieving a desired result. For many families, the desired result is to enable the older person to live as independently as possible for as long as possible, despite the older person's physical or mental limitations.
- Taking into consideration other responsibilities—such as family and work—as you make caregiving decisions.

THE RIGHT ATTITUDE

Effective caregiving starts with the right attitude—your outlook on life and your caregiving situation. The right attitude will see you through the many challenges of caregiving. Depending on your situation, those challenges may include time management, legal issues, financial pressures, providing hands-on care, conflicts with siblings, or finding the right services or the right type of housing.

The four principles on the next page describe a healthy attitude for effective caregiving.

FOUR PRINCIPLES FOR EFFECTIVE CAREGIVING

These four principles developed by the Caregiver Action Network (CAN)—formerly the National Family Caregivers Association—can help you maintain perspective amid the many challenges and changes you face in caring for your older family member—and balancing the work and family dimensions of life. Return to these principles at times of uncertainty and stress to regain perspective and balance. See the CAN website for other tips https://caregiveraction.org

#1. CHOOSE TO TAKE CHARGE OF YOUR LIFE

We often fall into caregiving because of an unexpected event. At some point, you need to step back and consciously say, "I choose to take on this caregiving role." Making this conscious choice goes a long way toward eliminating the feeling of being a victim.

#2. LOVE, HONOR, AND VALUE YOURSELF

Self-care isn't a luxury. It is a basic need of every human being. Step back and recognize just how extraordinary you are, and remember your own good health is the very best present you can give your loved one.

#3. SEEK, ACCEPT, AND, AT TIMES, DEMAND HELP

Caregiving, especially at its most intense levels, is definitely more than a one-person job. Asking for help is a sign of your strength and an acknowledgment of your abilities and your limitations.

#4. STAND UP AND BE COUNTED

Recognize that caregiving comes on top of being a parent, a child, a spouse. Honor your caregiving role. Speak up for your own well-deserved recognition and rights. Become your own advocate, both within your own immediate caregiving sphere and beyond.

© Caregiver Action Network https://caregiveraction.org (202) 454-3970 Caregiver Self-Advocacy: Four Messages to Live By

PART 2

SIX STEPS TO CAREGIVING/ WORK BALANCE

1. Assess your situation
2. Learn about resources
3. Weigh the options
4. Implement your plan
5. Monitor for changes
6. Adjust the plan

HOW TO GET THE MOST OUT OF THE SIX STEPS

Caregiving/work balance situations vary tremendously. No single action plan works for everyone. However, you can develop a strategy that works for you. You have options. You have rights. And you can tap resources to lighten the load.

Use these six steps to create your unique plan for balancing caregiving and work.

The same six steps apply both at work (your job responsibilities) and outside of work (your caregiving responsibilities).

Each step begins with an *At Work* section, followed by a *Caregiving* section.

To get the most out of each step, read through the *At Work* and *Caregiving* sections. Then, go back and complete the activities suggested under either *At Work* or *Caregiving*, depending on which area needs your attention first. Be sure to complete both sections before moving on to the next step.

At the end of each step, complete the *Summary Form*. These completed forms will give you a helpful one-page snapshot of your situation.

Writing information down makes your situation more manageable and gives you a valuable reference when you need to deal with your supervisor, co-workers, or others at work—as well as doctors, social workers, and others involved in the elder's care.

Use the forms included with each step to capture your thoughts and feelings in writing. Before you begin, you may wish to make copies of the forms, so you can use them again as your circumstances change and you update your plan.

STEP 1

ASSESS YOUR SITUATION

“ If you don't ask the right questions,
you don't get the right answers. ”
—Edward Hodnett

Whether you have been thrust into the role of caregiver due to a crisis in the elder's life or you have been involved in caring for someone for some time, you need good information to make good decisions—at work and outside of work.

You need to assess:

- Your work situation
- The caregiving situation, including:
    1. your view of it
    2. the elder's point of view
    3. basic information about the older person
    4. other family members' views

IF YOU ARE IN A CRISIS SITUATION RIGHT NOW...

If you need to focus your attention right now on making a critically important decision about the elder's health or well-being (e.g. your mother has been suddenly hospitalized—and is now being discharged), you may need approval to make phone calls while at work or take time off to resolve the crisis. If so, talk to the right person at work as soon as possible. If you are comfortable talking to the owner, your supervisor, or the manager of your unit, call or set up a meeting right away. In a larger organization, you may want to contact someone in human resources or employee relations.

- Explain that a seriously ill family member requires your attention.
- State that you may need to be absent from work with little or no advance notice over the next week or so until the crisis passes.
- Make a note of the name of the person to whom you speak, as well as the date and time of your conversation.
- Check your employer's policy on sick leave. Some employers allow paid time off for care of a relative who is sick.
- If the situation requires more than a few hours of your time away from work, you may be eligible for unpaid leave under the federal Family and Medical Leave Act (FMLA) which applies to organizations with 50 or more employees. See page 37 for information about FMLA. As of 2019, six states offer paid family leave: California, Massachusetts, New Jersey, New York, Rhode Island, and Washington state. For an up-to-date list of such state benefits, visit the website of the National Partnership for Women and Families: http://www.ncsl.org/research/labor-and-employment/paid-family-leave-resources.aspx
- Use the *Elder Care Resources from A-Z* section, beginning on page 77, as a quick reference to find the help you need.

When the crisis has passed, use the steps in this guide to work out a longer-term plan to balance your caregiving and work responsibilities.

STEP 1: ASSESS YOUR SITUATION

AT WORK

To create a workable plan, take charge of your work situation by assessing:

- The impact caregiving is having on your work
- The specifics of your job responsibilities
- The amount of flexibility in your work schedule
- The level of trust between you, your supervisor, and co-workers

Create a file folder where you can keep the documents you will create for your caregiving/work balance plan. Keep it secure. This is private information, for your use only.

Answer the questions under each of the headings below as honestly as possible. When you have completed these questions, write down the results on the *At Work Assessment Summary Form* on page 20.

FORM 1:

THE IMPACT CAREGIVING IS HAVING ON MY WORK

Circle a response below each statement.

Over the past three months, my involvement in elder care has:

1. Caused me to arrive late or leave work early more than once.

Agree   Disagree   Not sure

2. Required me to make phone calls related to elder care while at work.

Agree   Disagree   Not sure

3. Caused me to become tired or emotionally upset, resulting in feeling distracted at work.

Agree   Disagree   Not sure

4. Required me to take one or more days off from work.

Agree   Disagree   Not sure

5. Caused me to wonder whether I can continue to work my normally scheduled hours.

Agree   Disagree   Not sure

If you circled "Agree" to two or more questions above, caregiving is having a significant impact on your work. Note this on the *At Work Assessment Summary Form* on page 20.

MY JOB RESPONSIBILITIES

No one knows your job responsibilities better than you do.

To create a workable solution for caregiving/work balance, you need a clear picture of your job responsibilities. Knowing what is expected of you is an important step toward taking charge of your work life.

Do you have a written job description? If you do, is it up-to-date? Does it reflect what you actually do on a day-to-day basis? When was the last time you and your supervisor looked at the list of your responsibilities? If it is up to date: wonderful! Place a copy in your caregiving/work balance folder.

If you have a job description and it is not up to date, take it out now. Set aside some time when you will not be distracted. Go through the job description, point by point. Mark it up. Cross out the items that are no longer accurate. Be sure it includes every responsibility. Edit it to include needed changes. Be sure to include your hours of work, e.g.,

"Monday - Friday, 9–5," as well as today's date. Then, share a copy with a trusted co-worker and ask if he or she thinks it is accurate. Make any needed changes. Keep it handy for use in the next steps of this caregiving/work balance process.

If you don't have a job description, let's prepare one! Create a new document. At the top, write down what you believe your job title to be. Write down the name and title of the person to whom you report. Write down the heading "Responsibilities." Think about each important activity you perform in the course of a week or a month on your job. Write each one down, numbering each item. At the bottom of the page, write "Hours of Work" and state your normal work hours, e.g., "Monday - Friday, 9–5" Also, write down today's date. Share this document with a trusted co-worker and ask if he or she thinks it is accurate. Make any needed changes. Congratulations! You have just prepared a draft job description. Keep a copy handy for use in the next steps of this caregiving/work balance process.

Make a note regarding your job responsibilities on the *At Work Assessment Summary Form* on page 20. For your job description to be official, it needs to be approved by the person to whom you report.

FORM 2:

THE DEGREE OF FLEXIBILITY IN MY WORK SCHEDULE

In survey after survey, employees with caregving responsibilities have said that flexible work hours are a top concern. Assessing how much flexibility you have at work will help you define the options available to you.

Circle a response below each statement.

1. My job responsibilities do not require me to be at my desk or work location at all times during work hours (except for lunch and rest breaks).

     Agree   Disagree   Not sure

2. Someone in my department can cover for me if I need to be away from my regular work location for an hour or two.

     Agree   Disagree   Not sure

3. Other employees work flexible hours that allow them to vary their starting and leaving times.

     Agree   Disagree   Not sure

4. I work as part of a team. We share responsibilities and have the flexibility to cover for each other if one of us needs to take time off from work.

     Agree   Disagree   Not sure

5. My employer has a policy of allowing flexible work hours.

     Agree   Disagree   Not sure

If you circled Agree three or more times, you enjoy a flexible work environment. If you circle Disagree on most of the questions, you have limited options for flexibility. If you circled Not Sure for any item, you need to do more research to get accurate information. Record your results on the *At Work Assessment Summary Form* on page 20.

FORM 3:
THE LEVEL OF TRUST BETWEEN ME AND MY SUPERVISOR

Trust is the level of safeness we feel with another human being. Understanding the level of trust that exists in your place of work will help determine your course of action.

Circle a response below each statement.

1. My supervisor and I treat each other with respect and politeness.

Agree   Disagree   Not sure

2. My supervisor keeps commitments he or she has made to me.

Agree   Disagree   Not sure

3. I don't worry about making occasional mistakes on the job because my supervisor respects my work and sees mistakes as a way to learn and grow on the job.

Agree   Disagree   Not sure

4. I would be comfortable discussing my caregiving situation with my supervisor if I felt that caregiving was having an impact on my job performance.

Agree   Disagree   Not sure

If you circled Agree for three or more of questions 1-4, you have a moderate to high level of trust with the person to whom you report. If you circled Disagree for most items, the trust level needs improvement. Note your response on the *At Work Assessment Summary Form* on page 20.

USING THE AT WORK ASSESSMENT SUMMARY FORM

Write your comments on the *At Work Assessment Summary Form* on the next page. Include notes about your particular situation. You will refer to the completed form in the next steps in the caregiving/work balance process.

FORM 4:
AT WORK ASSESSMENT SUMMARY FORM

WORK PLACE FACTORS   Today's date: _____

MY ASSESSMENT

A. The impact of caregiving on my work performance over the past three months. Check one:

O High impact

O Some impact

O No impact

The most important way in which caregiving is affecting my job performance is:

_____

_____

Comments:

_____

_____

_____

_____

B. My job responsibilities. Status of my job description:

O I have no job description

O My job description is out of date

O My job description is up to date

O I updated my job description but haven't obtained approval yet

O I just created a job description and haven't obtained approval yet

Comments:

_____

_____

_____

C. The degree of flexibility in my work schedule. Check one:

    ○ I have a lot of flexibility in my work hours and schedule

    ○ I have limited flexibility

    ○ I have little or no flexibility

Comments:

_____

_____

_____

D. The level of trust between me, my supervisor, and co-workers. Check one:

    ○ High level of trust

    ○ Moderate level of trust

    ○ Low level of trust

Comments:

_____

_____

_____

STEP 1: ASSESS YOUR SITUATION

CAREGIVING

YOUR VIEW OF THE ELDER'S SITUATION: FEELINGS AND CONCERNS

A relationship with an older relative—especially with a parent—can be very stressful. Realizing that the independent, resourceful individual who looked after you and guided you may now need you to look after her can be upsetting and confusing for you and for the elder. And long after you think you have resolved old struggles or healed over hurt feelings, a casual comment or a certain gesture can trigger a flood of emotions.

Strong emotions are a part of caregiving. There will be times of joy, satisfaction, laughter, relief, peace, and reflection. And there will be tough times when "negative" emotions—hurt, fear, sadness, isolation, frustration, stress, guilt, anger, and confusion—seem to take over.

There is nothing wrong with feeling any of these emotions, positive or negative. It is healthy to allow ourselves all these feelings. It is how we act on our emotions that can cause trouble.

Sometimes, the more difficult emotions send signals or messages that we need to hear. For example, sometimes feelings of frustration or stress may mean that we need to re-think how we are doing something—or that we need to seek help from others.

It is not easy to keep your own emotions in check. And it is important to sort out your feelings from those of the older person and other members of the family.

Complete the questions on page 24 to identify your concerns.

THE OLDER PERSON'S POINT OF VIEW

Contrary to the popular phrase, you are not "parenting your parent." Elder care involves one adult caring for another adult. No matter how frail, the elder has the right to make choices about how and where to live and whether or not to accept help from others—to the extent that he or she is mentally capable of making such decisions.

In an effective caregiving relationship, the caregiver respects the autonomy and decision-making capacity of the elder. When the elder refuses help, feelings of anxiety and guilt may arise for you. When you are in a calm frame of mind, express your fears and concerns for his or her safety. You may need to leave it at that for a while. Know that you have done what you can do, for now. You can bring up the subject again after a while. The older person's feelings may change—or not. Your obligation is to make suggestions to improve the elder's circumstances. The older person retains the right to decide how to live his or her own life.

Heather and Bob were concerned about the ability of Heather's father, Richard, an 80-year-old retired teacher, to live safely at home after the death of Heather's mother, Greta. For years, Greta had tended to Richard's day-to-day needs, not because of any physical or mental incapacity, but because that's the way her role of wife had been defined over the years.

After Greta's death, Richard had begun to skip meals. He allowed house cleaning to slip to the point where things began looking disheveled. Yet, Richard rejected suggestions from Heather to engage the service of a homemaker to help with cleaning and meal preparation, saying "I know what I'm doing and I'm happy this way. I don't need any help."

Most importantly, from Heather and Bob's point of view, Richard had little interaction with other people and he refused to give up his smoking habit—a safety concern. Greta had served as the hub of the couple's social life, and, with her passing, Richard no longer attended the church-related events that kept the couple in touch with others.

Without consulting Richard, Heather researched assisted living residences in the area and found one that included some residents who were retired from the same school where Richard had taught for years. To their dismay, Richard angrily refused to even visit the residence, saying "I resent the fact that, suddenly, you're assuming you know what's best for me!" Regarding his daughter's concern about his smoking putting him at risk, Richard responded, "That's none of your concern. For me, smoking is one of life's small pleasures. I'm not about to give it up now."

Heather and Bob reluctantly came to the conclusion that they would need to learn to allow their own desire for peace of mind to take a back seat to Richard's right to autonomy in decision making—at least as long as he remained mentally competent.

FORM 5:
YOUR CAREGIVING CONCERNS

At any given point in our caregiving experience, we will perceive certain aspects of what is happening as more important than others. This exercise helps you identify what's most important to you right now.

Respond to the questions below. Follow up on items you answer "don't know."

1. How often does the older person socialize with others, compared to a year or two ago?

Less Often About the same More Often Don't know

2. How active is he/she with hobbies, interests, and regularly scheduled activities, compared to a year or two ago?

Less Often About the same More Often Don't know

3. How would you rate his/her ability to make use of transportation and neighborhood services?

Very limited ability Limited ability No limitation in ability Don't Know

4. Check each of the functional abilities below in which the elder has impairments:

O Vision
O Hearing
O Use of Arms
O Use of Legs
O Other: _____

5. Is he/she able to get in and out of bed unassisted?

Yes No Don't Know

6. Is he/she able to drive an automobile safely?

Yes No Don't Know

7. Is he/she showing signs of loss of memory?

      Yes   No   Don't Know

8. Does he/she drink alcohol?

      Yes   No   Don't Know

If yes, how many drinks per day? _____

Per week? _____

9. Does he/she have difficulty taking medications as prescribed?

      Yes   No   Don't Know

10. Name and phone number/email address of a person who would be able to help the elder in case of an emergency:

_____

_____

_____

_____

11. What is the current problem or issue from the elder's point of view?

_____

_____

_____

_____

12. What is the most important current problem or issue from your point of view?

_____

_____

_____

_____

FORM 6:
ARE YOU CUT OUT TO BE THE PRIMARY CAREGIVER?

Are you the best person to serve as primary caregiver, coordinating all aspects of the elder's care? It is healthy to seek and accept help—to share the caring with others, the "secondary" caregivers. It is essential, however, to have one person oversee the situation.

The skills needed to effectively manage the care of an elder are like those needed to successfully run a family business—with a healthy dose of human kindness added to the mix:

- managing the financial aspects of care,
- coordinating the actions of the people who are directly or indirectly involved,
- organizing the support of professionals like doctors and lawyers,
- managing relationships among those involved in care,
- arranging housing and transportation, and, in some cases,
- providing personal care like bathing or helping with dressing and undressing.

To get a sense as to whether or not you are cut out to be the primary caregiver, respond to each statement below as honestly as you can. For each statement, circle a number from 1 to 5, as follows:

1 = Disagree strongly, 2 = Disagree, 3 = Don't Know, 4 = Agree, 5 = Agree Strongly.

1. I know myself.

    1   2   3   4   5

2. I am aware of the impact I have on other people.

    1   2   3   4   5

3. I can accept weaknesses.

    1   2   3   4   5

4. I can identify strengths of others.

    1   2   3   4   5

5. I can accept people who are different from me or who think differently from me.

    1   2   3   4   5

6. I have a flexible personal style.

      1   2   3   4   5

7. I can create a trusting environment for people to think, work, and live in.

      1   2   3   4   5

8. I can manage conflict by active involvement in a positive way.

      1   2   3   4   5

If five or more of your answers rank in the 1-2 range, consider asking another member of your family to take on the role of primary caregiver or engaging the help of a professional geriatric care manager (see *Finding the Help You Need* on page 43).

If most of your responses are in the 4-5 range, you may be a good candidate for primary caregiver.

In either case, what's important is that you make a choice about what role you will play. Choosing to take charge of your life is the first principle of effective caregiving.

BASIC INFORMATION ABOUT THE OLDER PERSON

It is critically important to separate your feelings about your older loved one's situation from the facts regarding his or her condition.

You will want to have at your fingertips all the vital information on the following pages, so that you, the older person, and other family members can make good decisions and respond to changing circumstances.

HEALTH EXAMINATION

When was the last time the older person had a complete physical exam? If it has been more than two years, work with the elder to arrange a visit to the doctor. If you suspect the presence of Alzheimer's disease or other dementia, talk to the doctor to arrange an assessment.

Ask the older person for permission to accompany him/her on visits to the doctor, so that you have a common understanding of his or her health condition. Ask the elder sign a HIPAA release form (available from the doctor's office). This is legally required for you to access his/her healthcare information. Write down your concerns about particular conditions, including the elder's mental health, and bring them to the doctor's visit.

You may wish to arrange for an assessment by a physician who specializes in care of the elderly, known as a geriatrician. This can be helpful if the elder has multiple health problems or if there are concerns about signs of dementia, like disorientation or forgetfulness. To find a geriatrician in your local area, contact the *American Geriatrics Society* at (800) 247-4779 or visit www.healthinaging.org

SETTING UP AN INFORMATION FOLDER

- Buy a notebook or a three-ring binder or set up a file on your computer.
- Begin collecting all pertinent information in this one place.
- Keep your information folder in the same spot all the time, so you will know where to find it when you need it.

Make several copies of the completed "Information About the Older Person" on the following pages. It's easier and faster to hand a copy of the information to health care personnel than it is to repeat the same information over and over. It cuts down on errors, too.

FORM 7:
INFORMATION ABOUT THE OLDER PERSON

1. Name _____

2. Address

_____

_____

3. Telephone number _____

4. Date of birth _____

5. Social Security number _____

6. Medicare number _____

7. **Medicaid number** (if applicable) _____

8. Other health insurance, name of company, policy number

_____

_____

_____

9. Advance planning documents

    O Health care proxy   Location: _____

    O Living will   Location: _____

    O Durable power of attorney   Location: _____

    O Do Not Resuscitate (DNR) Order   Location: _____

10. Primary Caregiver name, relationship, address, phone, email address

_____

_____

_____

11. Primary doctor's name, address, telephone number

_____

_____

_____

12. Names, telephone numbers of specialist doctors caring for the older person

_____

_____

_____

13. List all medications the elder is taking

Medication: _____ Dose: _____ Frequency: _____

Medication: _____ Dose: _____ Frequency: _____

Medication: _____ Dose: _____ Frequency: _____

Medication: _____ Dose: _____ Frequency: _____

Medication: _____ Dose: _____ Frequency: _____

Medication: _____ Dose: _____ Frequency: _____

Medication: _____ Dose: _____ Frequency: _____

14. Physical impairments (hearing, vision impairment, confusion, problems with balance, etc.)

_____

_____

_____

15. Names, phone numbers, e-mail addresses of persons in regular touch with the older person (neighbors, friends, etc.)

_____

_____

_____

_____

16. Other agencies involved in assisting the elder (list for each: agency name, contact person, telephone number, fax number, e-mail address)

_____

_____

_____

17. Advisors: Attorney & Financial Advisor/Broker - names, addresses, phone, emails

_____

_____

_____

_____

18. Social Security (amount of monthly check) _____

19. Supplemental Security Income (SSI) (monthly) _____

20. Pension(s) (monthly) _____

21. Other income (rents/dividends/interest) _____

22. Total annual income (multiply the total of items 18-21 by 12) $ _____

23. Bank(s): names of institutions, account numbers

_____

_____

_____

_____

24. Life insurance policies—companies and policy numbers:

_____

_____

_____

_____

25. Location of other financial assets (annuities, stocks, bonds, etc.)

_____

_____

_____

_____

OTHER FAMILY MEMBERS: THEIR FEELINGS AND CONCERNS

The assessment of the caregiving situation needs to include information about the feelings and views of others who are concerned with the elder's well-being. This may include the elder's spouse, your siblings (if the elder is your parent), or a friend or relative with whom the elder has a close personal relationship.

If you are the primary caregiver, you may feel like you are doing too much—or that siblings and others are not doing enough. For their part, your siblings or others who are close to the elder may feel they are being shut out of the situation. Worse, they may not have any idea what to do to help you, so they just stay away.

Open up communications with others. At the start of caregiving, you may feel that no one else can care for the elder as well as you, but the burden can quickly grow too heavy for one person to handle. If you don't offer others a chance to help now, you may find that they will expect you to go it alone later.

Even if your brother hasn't visited dad in eight years, he needs to know if dad's health is deteriorating. He may or may not choose to act on the information, but he needs to be given the opportunity to make his views known. It is important to:

- Involve family members now. Consider holding a family meeting (see next page).

- Listen to the concerns expressed by siblings and others.

- Draft a "job description" for caregiving, listing all the tasks that need to be performed. Let your siblings help revise it, taking on some of the responsibilities. This helps everyone understand how to help.

- Keep them informed and up-to-date as the situation changes.

If you are not the primary caregiver, you may feel you are not doing enough. You may be relieved that you don't have to bear the burden of overseeing care. In any case, you can:

- Maintain or renew your relationship with the elder by visiting or calling regularly.

- Support the primary caregiver by offering to help in the ways you can, including monetary help.

- Be sure to thank the primary caregiver for the work he or she is doing.

- Lend a listening ear to the primary caregiver. Even if you don't have answers to the day-to-day dilemmas he or she faces, you can provide an opportunity for the primary caregiver to let off steam, thus helping to reduce feelings of stress and isolation.

HOLDING A FAMILY MEETING

Talk to the other members of your family—no matter how you feel about them. You can meet informally, for example, at a family gathering, or in a more formal setting.

WHO ATTENDS?

Keep the elder informed and involved in planning for care, to the extent that he or she is mentally capable. Initially, however, you may want a "siblings only" session so you can air issues and concerns without needlessly upsetting the older person. However, the purpose of such a meeting should not be to make decisions about what the older person is to do if the person is capable of participating. If you know a professional who can add expertise to the discussion (e.g., social worker, clergy) check first with other family members to get their OK to invite the professional.

HOW DOES A FAMILY MEETING WORK?

Select a facilitator who will keep the discussion focused on the elder's situation and make sure that everyone has a chance to have their say. A family member can serve as facilitator if that is comfortable for everyone. Include spouses of siblings if they are involved in helping.

Create an agenda: a list of questions, written down in advance by each of the participants. The facilitator builds these questions into the discussion. Some guidelines:

- Listen to each other. The value of the meeting is hearing what all members of the family have to say.

- As someone speaks, write down key points on a flip chart for all to see.

- Don't interrupt when another person is speaking. Hold questions or comments until after each person has had his or her say.

Start with a review of the facts and issues concerning the elder's situation and the outlook for his or her medical condition and ability to function independently. If the elder is present, listen to how he or she sees the situation. If the elder is not present, make sure someone has had a frank discussion with the parent beforehand, to really hear his or her wishes. Someone should summarize the older person's views. Then, open up a discussion of others' concerns.

Next, focus on what needs to be done now and in the near future. Write down a list of tasks and who will be responsible for performing them (e.g., researching local agencies, calling the elder daily, filling prescriptions). Plan to meet again in 30 to 60 days for an update.

One person will likely shoulder most of the responsibility as the primary caregiver. Making the effort now to share the caring can prevent feelings of resentment later.

STEP 2

LEARN ABOUT RESOURCES

> " It is what we know already that
> often prevents us from learning. "
> —Claude Bernard

Take the time to learn about the benefits and supports available to you before you are in a crisis situation.

STEP 2: LEARN ABOUT YOUR RESOURCES

AT WORK

If you completed the *At Work Summary Assessment Form* in Step One (page 20), you have a good sense of:

- How your caregiving situation now affects your work—or if it's a future concern,
- Your list of job responsibilities,
- The amount of flexibility in your work schedule, and
- The level of trust you feel with your supervisor and co-workers.

TALK TO OTHERS

It is important to let your manager and your close co-workers know what is going on so they provide support. When caregiving requires you to take time off, or causes you to give less than 100 percent at work, people will notice. If you don't share information about your situation, others may think you are simply not pulling your weight. Some co-workers may feel resentful. You may set yourself up for a poor performance appraisal—which will hurt your chances of getting help.

If you are not comfortable bringing up the subject with your supervisor, consider contacting Human Resources, the Employee Assistance Program (EAP), or Employee Relations staff at your work place. See information on these below.

WORKPLACE RESOURCES

Identify the workplace supports described below that are available in your workplace. If you are not sure if a particular support is available, make a note to contact your supervisor or the human resources department to inquire about it.

Dependent Care Assistance Plan (DCAP)—is a tax-favored arrangement by which the employer reimburses employees for dependent care expenses, makes payments to third parties for care of employees' dependents, or provides a dependent care facility for employees. If you need to purchase elder care in order to remain gainfully employed, you may be able to take advantage of this tax-saving plan, provided you and the elder live in the same home. The DCAP application will require you to anticipate and state the amount you will spend in advance of the year during which you will incur the expenses. Using pre-tax dollars to pay for services like home care or adult day care can save you a substantial amount of money each year.

Direct Service Help—A few employers offer services at the work site, like adult day care or family caregiver support groups, or will pay some or all of the cost for geriatric care management or emergency back-up home care. See the *Elder Care Resources—from A-Z* section on page 77 for descriptions of these services.

Betty is an account manager at a CPA firm. Her mother lives nearby and is homebound due to coronary heart disease. Recently, the home care agency called the night before cancelling the home care aide visit scheduled for the next morning. Betty was scheduled to make an important presentation to a client's executive management team the next morning. Under an arrangement put into place by her employer for back-up home care, Betty was able to call an agency engaged by her employer and set up the needed visit for the next morning. She made the presentation, with the peace of mind of knowing her mother was receiving needed help. The employer paid half the cost of the emergency back-up home care visit.

Employee Assistance Programs (EAP)—Provide counseling and advice on family matters, sometimes including elder care. The employer provides an "800" number to call and help can be provided over the phone or at in-person counseling sessions.

Donna's father has a history of alcoholism. After not drinking for several years, Donna noticed on her last visit to his home (on the other coast), that he was definitely drinking again. This stirred up powerful emotions in Donna—and unpleasant memories from her childhood. Before starting to help her dad, she needed to sort out her own feelings. She made an appointment with an Employee Assistance Program counselor who helped her gain perspective on the situation.

Employee Relations Specialists—Some human resource departments include an employee relations specialist who serves as a resource to employees and managers in preventing or resolving employment-related conflicts. If you cannot discuss or resolve a caregiving/work conflict issue with your supervisor, contact the human resources staff to find out who can listen to your concerns and serve as a mediator between you and the manager to find a mutually satisfactory solution.

Family and Medical Leave Act (FMLA)—This federal law applies to organizations with 50 or more employees. FMLA guarantees that employees can take up to 12 weeks of unpaid leave a year to care for a newborn, a newly adopted child, or for a seriously ill parent, spouse, or child, or to recover from their own serious health conditions. In addition, it provides job protections and continued health insurance coverage. FMLA job protection lasts for 12 weeks during any given year, so long as the employee is not out of work for more than 12 weeks total during the year.

The 12 weeks of leave need not be taken consecutively. Leave may be taken in shorter increments, if needed. For example, you can take two weeks off to assist a parent who has returned home from the hospital following heart surgery, and then two additional weeks later in the year if she should require you to be at home to help her to learn to use medical equipment related to her recovery.

For more information about FMLA, visit the website of the National Partnership for Women and Families at www.nationalpartnership.org and click on Workplace Equity, or the U.S. Department of Labor (DOL) at https://www.dol.gov/general/topic/benefits-leave/fmla or call the DOL Wage and Hour Division Referral Line at 1-866-4-USA-DOL and request the number of your local office of the Wage and Hour Division. The local office will send you a free copy of the DOL fact sheet on FMLA. Some State laws go beyond FMLA requirements and provide additional benefits. For a state-by-state listing, visit http://www.nationalpartnership.org/our-work/workplace/paid-leave.html.

Some States Offer Paid Family Leave—As of 2019, the following states have enacted Paid Family Leave (PFL) laws: California, the District of Columbia, Massachusetts, New Jersey, New York, Rhode Island, and Washington state. These laws generally cover individuals who take time off to care for a seriously ill family member or bond with a new minor child. PFL generally allow for a certain number of weeks of paid leave in a twelve-month period. Benefits equal a defined percentage of earnings and have a maximum benefit per week. For details on provisions of these laws visit the website of the National Partnership for Women and Families http://www.nationalpartnership.org/our-work/workplace/paid-leave.html.

Flexible Work Policies—Flextime refers to work schedules that permit employees to choose their starting and quitting times within limits set by management. Your employer may have a formal policy that limits flextime to certain job categories or requires submission of a formal request for a flextime arrangement. In a recent survey, 73% of major employers offered some form of flextime.

> Terry's 90-year-old aunt, Annie, lives with her. Annie can't be left home alone all day, so she attends an adult day center five days a week. Because her employer allows Terry, an administrative assistant, to arrive at 9:30 and leave at 5:30 (rather than the normal 9-5 hours), she is able to be at home to assist Annie in getting into and out of the wheelchair-equipped van that transports her to and from the day center.

Informational Seminars—Provide specific information and skills development for employees involved with elder care. Talk with someone in your human resources department about inviting speakers in to talk about caregiving issues.

Barbara attended a lunch time workshop in the company conference room. A social worker from an Area Agency on Aging described housing options for elders. She learned that her father's income would probably disqualify him for senior housing. She obtained the names of three assisted living facilities that might make sense in a year or two. After the seminar, she requested information from each and arranged to visit before the need was critical. She chose one and placed a deposit to get her father on the waiting list.

Resource and Referral Service—Provides employees, and sometimes retirees, with access, via phone or web portal, to personalized consultation about caregiving issues, including information about services, lists of specific providers in the elder's local community, assistance in formulating alternative plans of action, and help in contacting and arranging services. There is usually no fee for the employee.

Mike's position as an attorney in the legal department of a major bank makes intense demands on his time. His father, who lives 400 miles away, needed some short-term help with meal preparation and housekeeping during his recuperation from an operation. Mike and his family appreciated the help of the telephone counselor at the company's Elder Care Resource and Referral Service. She listened well, found two home care providers in his dad's town, and arranged for the needed help.

Telecommuting (also known as working from home, or e-commuting)—A work arrangement in which the employee works outside the office, often working from home or a location close to home (including coffee shops, libraries, and various other locations).

Jerry's sister Linda is the primary caregiver for their mother, Rose, whose Parkinson's disease has restricted her to home. She can walk slowly but needs to be monitored to avoid falling. Because Jerry's employer allows him to work away from the office two mornings a week, Linda can count on those hours to get out of the house while Jerry works from home. She can run errands or give herself a breather. Jerry, a regional sales representative, brings along his laptop and uses the time to call contacts, schedule appointments, and prepare correspondence and reports.

FOLLOW UP NOTES:

I will speak to my supervisor or contact Human Resource to learn more about these work place resources:

_____

_____

_____

_____

_____

_____

_____

_____

STEP 2: LEARN ABOUT YOUR RESOURCES

CAREGIVING

Now that you have collected basic information about the elder and clarified your own concerns and those of other family members, including the elder herself, you need information about what kinds of help are available in the community where the older person lives.

Just because an elder is showing signs of frailty or reduced ability to perform some daily tasks does not mean that he or she necessarily needs to move to an assisted living facility or a nursing home. There are more home care and community care options available today than ever before—both for older people and the family members caring for them.

The telephone numbers and website addresses listed below can speed your search—once you know what you are looking for. The challenge is to find the right service or housing option, at the right time, at the right price.

TEN TIPS FOR NAVIGATING THE ELDER CARE SYSTEM

1. **Keep a written log**—in a computer file or a paper notebook—of your contacts with agencies and health care personnel. If you use a notebook, keep it readily at hand.

2. **Document phone calls:** names, dates and times called, phone numbers, key decisions.

3. **If you are not sure you understand something a professional says, ask him or her to repeat it.** If you are still not clear about it, ask again. It's your right to be well informed.

4. **Make several copies of the elder's basic health and insurance information** (see pages 29 – 32). Bring copies with you to medical appointments, hospital visits, and conversations with service providers to avoid having to repeat the same information over and over.

5. **Keep your cool dealing with bureaucrats and health care professionals.** You may need their help again in the not-too-distant future. Before making a telephone call that you know will be stressful, take a few deep breaths, compose yourself, and visualize a peaceful, positive outcome.

6. **Know where the older person's important papers are located:** bank books, checking account information, insurance policies, will, advance directives, and medical information. Scattered about? Put them in one place.

7. **Know your loved one's wishes before a crisis**, especially his or her feelings about taking extraordinary measures to prolong life in critical situations. Discuss these issues while he or she is lucid and able to communicate. For help in talking about these matters, use these resources: Five Wishes advance directive program of *Aging with Dignity*: Call 1-(888)-5-WISHES; www.agingwithdignity.org and Caring Conversations of the *Center for Practical Bioethics* 1-(800)-344-3829 www.practicalbioethics.org. Make sure directives are up-to-date, signed, and legal. Know where they are kept in the home.

8. **Make sure you have permission to speak with healthcare professionals on behalf of the elder.** The federal HIPAA law requires you to obtain a release form signed by the elder in order to access his or her health information. Health care professionals can provide a copy of this form.

9. **Tap the world of information on the Internet.** Research housing and service options and costs, take advantage of free resources and caregiver tips, and explore online support groups. Good starting points: Caregiver Action Network https://caregiveraction.org; Family Caregiving Alliance https://www.caregiver.org; National Alliance for Caregiving https://www.caregiving.org.

10. **Take care of yourself.** Take advantage of stress-reduction workshops and other preventive health services online or in person. Check out what's offered by your health plan and local community agencies like hospitals and community centers.

FINDING THE HELP YOU NEED

HOW DO YOU BEGIN?

You have two options for sorting through the service and program possibilities:

1. Do it yourself. Make use of the vast information on the Internet. Tap publicly funded specialists in aging information who are available to assist you (see *Elder Care Locator – Your Connection to the Aging Network* next page). Make use of elder supports your employer may offer, like a Resource and Referral Service (page 39).

2. Engage a care manager to do it for you. See Geriatric Care Managers on the next page.

In either case, educate yourself about the basic programs and service options that exist.

Take time now to review:

- Key Connections on the next page,
- The Importance of Planning Ahead on page 45, and
- *Elder Care Resources – from A-Z* beginning on page 77.

KEY CONNECTIONS

ELDERCARE LOCATOR—

YOUR CONNECTION TO THE AGING SERVICES NETWORK

Persons over 60 years of age, and family members who care for them, are eligible to receive free assistance in finding elder care programs and services through the national aging network, overseen by the federal *Administration on Aging*. It includes a *State Unit on Aging* in every state and over 600 *Area Agencies on Aging* (AAA's) serving every community in the nation. Trained AAA staff, called information and referral specialists, maintain extensive listings of local programs and services. They can, for example, tell you whether the older person is eligible to receive an in-home assessment of his or her condition through a publicly-funded case management program. To find your local AAA, contact the national *Elder Care Locator*:

- Call: 1-(800)-677-1116
- Visit: www.eldercare.gov

GERIATRIC CARE MANAGERS

A geriatric care manager is a professional, usually a social worker or nurse, who specializes in assisting older people and their families in making long-term care arrangements. Starting with an in-home visit, he or she can evaluate the elder's situation, recommend a plan of action, and even arrange and monitor services. Ask for proof of certification. Fees are usually paid privately. In some areas, publicly-funded care management may be available, depending on the elder's finances (see *Elder Care Locator*, above).

- Call: 1-(520)-881-8008 for the *Aging Lifecare Association* which maintains a listing of geriatric care managers throughout the U.S.
- Visit: https://www.aginglifecare.org

VOLUNTARY HEALTH ORGANIZATIONS

There is no substitute for talking to someone else dealing with the same issues you face. Some issues are disease specific. A caregiver helping someone with Multiple Sclerosis has different issues than one caring for someone with Alzheimer's disease. Voluntary health organizations, like the *National Multiple Sclerosis Society* or the *Alzheimer's Association*, can link you to professionals and volunteers—sometimes even other family caregivers—who know the ins and outs of coping with the progression and effects of the disease. See page 100 for a listing of voluntary health organization contacts.

THE IMPORTANCE OF PLANNING AHEAD

Medicare, the federal health insurance program for the elderly and disabled, does not pay for long term care. While Medicare does pay for most hospital and physician services (see program description *Elder Care Resources—from A-Z* on page 77), it pays only for short-term nursing home care after a hospital stay or for short-term, medically necessary, recuperative home health care. Medicaid, the state/federal program that covers healthcare for the poor and low-income elderly, pays for about 45% of all nursing home care costs in the U.S., according to the Center for Retirement Research.

Families and individuals pay out-of-pocket for about 75% of all long-term care (institutional and in-home). Many families come to this rude awakening when an older relative needs on-going assistance with tasks like preparing meals, household cleaning, bathing, dressing, or personal grooming. The annual average cost of nursing home care—$92,000 for a private room and $82,000 for a semi-private room—can quickly drain the typical family's financial resources. Assisted living costs about half as much. And, although in-home care can be less costly, around-the-clock care at home can cost as much as nursing home care.

Planning ahead for long term care help is vitally important. If your family has not looked into options like long term care insurance, life care communities, home equity conversion (also known as reverse mortgages), and other ways to prepare for future long-term care costs, the time to do it is now. Putting off planning will mean fewer choices tomorrow—when your older relative needs assistance. Some good sources of information:

- *AARP* Consumer Guide to Long Term Care Planning:
  https://states.aarp.org/aarp-resource-guide-for-long-term-care-planning/.

- The *National Association of Health Underwriters*: Consumer Guide to Long Term Care Planning:
  https://nahu.org/looking-for-an-agent/helpful-guides/consumer-guide-to-long-term-care.

- The *National Council on the Aging* (NCOA) maintains a website that provides a free, easy-to-use listing of thousands of State and federally-funded programs for older persons. By completing a single, confidential form online, you can determine eligibility for all these resources. NCOA continuously updates information in the database. Visit www.benefitscheckup.com.

Now, turn to *Elder Care Resources—From A-Z*, beginning on page 77, to learn more about the range of benefits, programs, and services available to you and your loved one.

STEP 3

WEIGH YOUR OPTIONS

> **"** It's easy to make good decisions when there are no bad options. **"**
> —Robert Half

STEP 3: WEIGH YOUR OPTIONS

AT WORK

In steps one and two, you assessed your work situation and researched the resources available at your place of employment. Now, you will create a list of possible solutions, then narrow the list down to a workable plan for you.

- If your caregiving situation is not strongly affecting your job performance now, use this step as an opportunity to plan ahead for future needs and minimize conflict.

- If you are feeling the impact of caregiving at work, the goal is to prepare a written request for a meeting with your supervisor.

In answering the questions below, refer to the documents in your Work/Life balance folder:

- The completed *At Work Summary Assessment Form*,

- Your job description—or list of job responsibilities, and

- Your list of work place resources that may be of help.

Don't worry if you haven't written down every last bit of information on each of these forms. If you have some information in each area, you are prepared for this step. Note any questions that remain unanswered.

MATCHING YOUR NEEDS WITH RESOURCES AT WORK

- Review the completed *At Work Summary Assessment Form* on page 20 and your follow up notes about workplace resources on page 36.

- Review the three documents in your Work/Life Balance folder.

- Read over your answers to the questions in steps one and two related to Caregiving.

- Then, follow these steps:

1. Use the table below to list the specific activities related to caregiving that now affect—or will soon affect—your performance at work. Fill in information about each activity. See the sample below.

FORM 8:
CAREGIVING ACTIVITIES AFFECTING MY WORK

SAMPLE

CAREGIVING ACTIVITY	HOW OFTEN DOES THIS ACTIVITY AFFECT MY WORK?	WHAT I NEED IN ORDER TO DEAL WITH THIS
Need to get mom "up and going" each morning	*Daily. I've been late for work 3 times in past two weeks.*	*Start work 30 minutes later. Possibly take a shorter lunch break, so I can leave at regular time.*

CAREGIVING ACTIVITY	HOW OFTEN DOES THIS ACTIVITY AFFECT MY WORK?	WHAT I NEED IN ORDER TO DEAL WITH THIS

2. Check off each of the workplace resources listed below that might help you deal with your situation. Write in your comments about each. For descriptions of these resources, see pages 36-39.

CO-WORKERS

My co-worker(s) could help me by (check all that apply):

○ Listening to me and providing emotional support.

○ Job-sharing with me. I can adjust or reduce my hours and have a co-worker share my job during the hours that I am not working.

○ Team coverage. I can arrange with other members of my team to cover my responsibilities at the beginning, end, or middle of the day, to accommodate my caregiving needs. I will cover their responsibilities at other times.

○ Co-worker coverage. A co-worker can cover my responsibilities temporarily while I address caregiving issues. Example: receptionist in another department handles my reception duties when I need to go to the doctor with dad.

○ Other: _____

Name(s) of co-workers who can provide support:

_____

_____

_____

_____

_____

Comments:

_____

_____

_____

_____

MY SUPERVISOR OR MANAGER

My supervisor or manager could help me by (check all that apply):

○ Listening to me and providing emotional support (if you feel the trust level exists)

○ Considering a request from me to adjust my work schedule

○ Allowing me to use some time at work to make caregiving-related phone calls

○ Allowing me to do some of my work at home

○ Other: _____

Comments:

_____

_____

_____

_____

RESOURCE AND REFERRAL SERVICE

Comments:

_____

_____

_____

_____

DEPENDENT CARE ASSISTANCE PLAN (DCAP)

Comments:

_____

_____

_____

_____

EMPLOYEE ASSISTANCE PROGRAM (EAP)

Comments:

_____

_____

_____

_____

HUMAN RESOURCES DEPARTMENT—EMPLOYEE RELATIONS SPECIALIST

Comments:

_____

_____

_____

_____

FAMILY AND MEDICAL LEAVE ACT (FMLA)

Comments:

_____

_____

_____

_____

FLEXIBLE WORK POLICIES

Comments:

_____

_____

_____

_____

INFORMATIONAL SEMINARS

Comments:

_____

_____

_____

_____

TELECOMMUTING

Comments:

_____

_____

_____

_____

3. You have identified the resources that can help you. If you need more information about any of them, call and obtain it now. Make a list of the actions you are considering.

4. If any of the actions you identified require the cooperation and support of co-workers, talk to them now. Discuss these points with them:

   - Your caregiving problem. (Be brief. Just the basics will do)

   - The changes you need to make at work in order to deal with the problem.

   - How long you expect the situation to last, e.g., Do you need some flexibility for the next 2-3 weeks—or is this a change that could last indefinitely?

   - The specific actions you would like each co-worker to take.

   - Suggest a trial period for the arrangement, so everyone knows when it will be evaluated. A one-month trial period is reasonable if you believe there will be a long-term need.

   - Explain that you need their input and support before you propose the change to your manager or supervisor.

   - Ask for a response by a certain date. One week is reasonable.

5. Based on your review of your needs and the resources available to you, make a list of the options you might pursue. Discuss your options with a trusted friend or relative.

6. Choose the best option. Write a brief description of the option you have chosen. We will refer to this description in the next step: Implement a Plan.

STEP 3: WEIGH YOUR OPTIONS

CAREGIVING

You have collected information about the elder and your family situation and gathered information about the specific programs and services that you feel could make a positive difference in the situation. Now, it's time to weigh alternative courses of action.

Use the *Caregiving Options Form* (next page) to write down possible courses of action.

1. **Refer to materials you have already prepared:**

    - Basic Information sheet about the elder
    - Notes from family meetings or conversations
    - Your caregiving log book of contacts with agencies, etc.

2. **At the top of the form:** Fill in today's date and a description of the area of concern. This can be health related, like Mom's Forgetfulness, or it can relate to some aspect of care, like Housing or Home Care Services, or it can relate to your own needs, like Adjusting My Daily Schedule. Make copies of the form and use one copy for each area of concern that you have.

3. **Row 1 (Issues/Concerns):** Considering all the information you've collected, write down in Column 1 a short phrase that describes the issue or problem that needs to be addressed. Be as specific as possible. For example, rather than writing "safety concerns," write "mom cannot safely use the bathroom."

4. **Row 2 (Options for Action):** Write down the ideas you have considered for addressing each issue or concern you listed in Column 1. For example, if mom cannot safely use the bathroom, you may be considering a.) installing grab bars near the toilet and in the bathtub, b.) buying or renting a commode that can be placed closer to her bed or chair, or c.) looking into the availability of a handicapped-accessible apartment in local senior housing. Write down each of the options and leave some space in between each.

5. **Row 3 (Pluses and Minuses):** For each of the possible actions or services you listed in Column 2, write down a plus sign (+) with each positive aspect and a negative sign (-) for each negative. For example, the option of adding grab bars might have a plus (+) because mom can continue to live at home and a (-) because you don't know who would do the installation.

6. **Row 4:** Note information you need to collect or concerns you didn't consider earlier, e.g., Contact the *Area Agency on Aging* or a website like Angie's List (www.angieslist.com) for a list of reputable contractors.

FORM 9:
CAREGIVING OPTIONS

Date: _____   Area of Concern: _____

1. THE ISSUES OR CONCERNS THAT NEED TO BE ADDRESSED.	2. OPTIONS: ACTIONS OR SERVICES THAT CAN ADDRESS THE CONCERNS	3. PLUSES (+) AND MINUSES (-) OF EACH ACTION OR SERVICE	4. UNANSWERED QUESTIONS AND ADDITIONAL INFORMATION NEEDED

Once you have completed a *Caregiving Options Form* for each of the issues and concerns, you will have a clearer idea of what needs to be done. Use the information to discuss the options with the elder and with other family members. Listen to their points of view.

Ideally, a consensus will emerge among family members about what to do and you can move on to implementing a plan. Sometimes, however, you may not have a consensus. If you are the primary caregiver, you may need to take the action that you feel is best. This can involve difficult, but necessary, choices. However, if you have followed the previous steps, you can proceed with confidence, knowing that you have considered the views of all concerned. Using your best judgment, take the needed actions and keep others informed.

STEP 4

IMPLEMENT YOUR PLAN

"To plan is human—to implement, divine! "
—Anonymous

STEP 4: IMPLEMENT YOUR PLAN

AT WORK

Congratulations! You have assessed your work situation, researched work place and community resources available to help you find a better balance between caregiving and work, weighed your options, and selected a course of action. You have a plan!

THREE TIPS FOR IMPLEMENTING YOUR PLAN

1. **Talk to people at work.** Your co-workers can provide helpful perspective and support.

2. **Consider the employer's viewpoint.** When you tell your manager what you need, show that you also understand your manager's responsibilities and your department's goals. You are more likely to obtain a positive result if you can talk about both your needs and the organization's objectives as they relate to your position.

3. **Continue to add to your work/life balance file.** Make notes in your file, keeping track of what is and is not working—as well as the dates of any important actions that you take, e.g. filing applications for specific benefits, meetings with your supervisor.

If your plan does not require approval from a manager or supervisor, you can begin to take needed actions now.

A WRITTEN REQUEST TO YOUR SUPERVISOR

If the option you chose requires management approval, now is the time to prepare a written request. Address it to the manager who works with you on a day-to-day basis. If it is ignored or denied, you may have the option of going to human resources or to a higher-level manager.

Your goal is an in-person meeting to discuss your request. Later, we suggest ways to arrange and conduct such a meeting. A sample written request is included on the next page.

Items to include in a written request to your manager or supervisor:

1. Your name and job title

2. Today's date

3. Description of the change you are proposing and the reason(s) why it is important

4. Statement about your current work load and goals of your department

5. Information about how the proposed change would affect the work of others

6. Statement regarding the support/cooperation of others in your department, if you have obtained this

7. Reference any organization policy or employee benefit that applies

8. Describe any change this would make to your job description

9. Proposed trial period for the change (start date, review date)

10. Date by which you would like a response in writing

11. Statement about your openness to other options

SAMPLE WRITTEN REQUEST TO SUPERVISOR

Your name and job title

Today's date

To: Mary K. Jones, Manager of Customer Relations
From: Jim Sussman, Customer Relations Representative
Re: Request for temporary change in hours of work
Date: May 1, 2022

Describe the change you are proposing and why it's important

I am writing to request a meeting to discuss a proposed change in my work schedule. I am making this proposal because I want to find a way to continue fulfilling my responsibilities here in the Customer Relations Department while dealing with an important family matter at home: arranging needed care for my mother who is recovering from surgery.

I propose that, for the next two months, my hours of work be more flexible. Specifically, I would like to work five core hours every day, from 10:00 - 3:00, with the flexibility to arrive later or leave earlier each day, as needed, to be available to assist my mother with her health care needs. I would continue to work a full 40-hour work week during this period, putting in the additional three hours each day at various times. I will keep a daily record of my hours worked.

Your current workload and the department's goals

I realize that we are all working together to continue to meet our and the department's goal of responding to each customer inquiry within one business day. My workload has been full but stable over the past quarter, as you know from my last performance evaluation. The change in hours will not interfere with my ability to meet my goals for volume of calls handled and quality of response to customers.

Effect on the work of others—and their support for the change

I spoke with Mary and Jay, the other members of my customer service team. They support my proposal. Since I will work the same total number of hours, they are willing and able to respond to calls during the hours I am not there. I will, in turn, cover for them during their normal 12:00 - 1:00 lunch hour.

Reference policy (flex-time guidelines)
Reference your job description
Propose trial period dates

This change fits within the flex-time guidelines that the human resources department issued last Spring. There would be no change to my job description. I would like to begin the new flexible work schedule next Monday, May 8 and try it out for one month—say through June 15. We can meet to evaluate how it is working out on June 15.

Include response date
Leave the door open for other solutions

I would like to meet with you later this week to discuss this. I am open to other ideas you might have for ways that I can continue to work as a member of the team in this department while dealing with my mother's health needs at home. I would appreciate your response before the end of the week, so we can set a time to meet. Thanks.

A MEETING WITH YOUR SUPERVISOR

After developing the written request, arrange to meet in person with your manager or supervisor to discuss it. The goals for a meeting are to 1) be sure that he or she understands what you are proposing, 2) obtain feedback on the contents of the written request, including suggestions for other solutions to your caregiving/work balance issues, and 3) obtain approval from him or her for the agreed-upon changes to your schedule or job description. Some suggestions for arranging and conducting a meeting:

- Tell your supervisor the purpose of the meeting.
- Have more than one date and time in mind to accommodate his/her schedule.
- Provide at least two business days' notice.
- Provide a copy of your proposal for his/her review in advance of the meeting.
- Try for a morning meeting time when you are both likely to have more energy and fewer distractions.

AT THE MEETING

- Begin by acknowledging the current goals and work situation in your department.
- Focus on the points in your written proposal. Review the proposal point by point.
- Ask for feedback and suggestions.
- Note any suggestions for additional information he/she may request.
- Request an answer by a certain date.

AFTER THE MEETING

- Prepare notes of what occurred at the meeting. Keep them in your work/life file.
- Get back to your supervisor with any additional information he/she may have requested.
- Follow up with a call or a note after the agreed-upon time for a decision.
- Be polite but firm in requesting a decision.

If you do not obtain an answer or your proposal is denied, consider taking up the matter with someone in the human resources department or with the person to whom your supervisor reports. If you decide to talk to a higher-level manager, inform your supervisor of your intention before doing so. Courtesy and persistence pay off.

STEP 4: IMPLEMENT YOUR PLAN

CAREGIVING

Now, it is time to take action on the plan you developed in Step 3.

- Use your information folder to keep track of all phone calls and correspondence with the agencies or programs you contact.

- Set a timeframe for implementing the plan. For example, if your older relative has had trouble with food shopping and preparation of meals and you decide to arrange for a daily home delivered meal, check in after a week to get first impressions of how the new service is working. Evaluate the situation in a month or two, to determine if new needs have arisen.

- Obtain and use the resources/publications listed in the *Elder Care Resources—from A-Z* section. These often include checklists that can help you sort through factors like cost, service quality standards, and consumer protections.

- If you do not see the elder in person on a regular basis, keep in touch with people who do, whether it is the home delivered meals driver, the care manager from an agency providing home care, or a neighbor who stops in to share a cup of coffee.

WHEN THE OLDER PERSON REFUSES HELP

You and your family can create what seems like the perfect solution to the problems facing the older person—even gaining the elder's tentative approval for needed changes. And then, when it comes time to make the move, or renovate the bathroom, or start the new home care service, the older person has a change of heart, refuses the help, or rejects the change to which you all agreed.

You can try strategies like convincing the elder to accept the new arrangement on a trial basis or finding a peer or trusted advisor, like the older person's doctor, to persuade the older person of the wisdom of the change. But, in the end, if the elder does not wish to implement the "perfect plan," you must respect his or her decision unless he or she is mentally incompetent.

Over the past year, Nancy noticed that her mother Jane's vision was fading fast. Jane was a diabetic and the disease was taking its toll. Yet, despite the fact that Jane could barely make her way from room to room, she refused to accept any help with chores like cooking or cleaning. With the demands of raising three children and working a 40+ hour per week job, Nancy did not have the time or energy to prepare meals and make the daily visits that she felt her mother needed.

On the advice of a friend, Nancy asked her mother if she would accept the help of a homemaker three times a week, not for her (Jane's) but for the sake of her daughter's (Nancy's) peace of mind. On this basis, Jane agreed to the homemaker help on a "trial" basis. But, on the day of the homemaker's first visit, Jane had a change of heart and refused to allow the homemaker to enter the house.

Finally, Nancy turned to her mother's long-time personal doctor. He spoke to Jane at her next visit and, at Nancy's request, told Jane that she must have some help with cooking and cleaning and that he had told Nancy to arrange for the homemaker to return the next day. To Nancy's surprise (and exasperation), her mother told her the next evening, "Doctor Wagner told me I needed a little help. And, you know, he was right! I always know I can trust Doctor Wagner to look out for my health."

STEP 5

MONITOR FOR CHANGES

" They must often change,
who would be constant in
happiness or wisdom. "
—Confucius

STEP 5: MONITOR FOR CHANGES

AT WORK

Once you have made a change in your work arrangement, keep track of how well it is working, not only from your point of view, but from the perspective of your co-workers and supervisor as well.

- Stick to the agreed-upon trial period.

- Talk to others regularly about how the arrangement is working out—before the end of the trial period.

- Keep notes in your work/life folder. What is working? What problems have cropped up? Be as specific as possible in your notes and record the dates on which important incidents (positive or negative) occur.

As the end of the trial period nears, ask yourself:

- Has this arrangement achieved what you hoped? (i.e., is it making it easier to balance work and caregiving responsibilities?)

- What feedback have you received from co-workers and your supervisor?

- Has your caregiving situation changed? If so, does the arrangement still make sense—or does it need to be modified in some way?

- Have your work responsibilities changed? Has your work load changed? Has the volume or type of work done in your department changed?

- Have any unexpected factors entered into the picture?

- Do you wish to continue the arrangement? If so, for what period of time?

STEP 5: MONITOR FOR CHANGES

CAREGIVING

Once the new plan is in place, watch for any significant changes in the older person's health or ability to function on a day-to-day basis. Changes can take place gradually or a crisis can arise overnight.

What specific kinds of changes should you look for? Key behaviors to keep an eye on include:

- Dramatic changes in sleeping or eating habits
- Noticeable increase in forgetfulness
- Decrease in ability to perform tasks like cooking, personal grooming
- Evidence of changes in personal hygiene or presence of incontinence
- Increase in the number of falls

If you live nearby, visit as regularly as you can. Vary the time of day or day of the week you visit so you can get a sense of how the elder is coping with the different aspects of daily routine.

If you live at a distance, work with someone in the elder's community who will check in regularly. If the older person is reasonably healthy and independent, you may be able to rely on a neighbor, friend or volunteer companion. If the elder is frail, you may feel more comfortable knowing that a professional regularly pays a visit. This can be arranged through a publicly-funded agency that offers case management if the elder is eligible for such assistance. Otherwise, you may want to engage a private geriatric care manager (see page 44) to check in and provide regular reports

If significant changes occur, you need to take a fresh look at the plan you created in steps 3 and 4. Consider whether the current living arrangement and types of assistance are still appropriate given the new circumstances.

Keep other family members and loved ones aware of what is happening. And share your impressions with the older person. He or she may not be aware of gradual declines in functioning that are taking place. Communicating with the elder about your concerns as changes occur can prevent the need for sudden confrontations in the future.

STEP 6

ADJUST THE PLAN OVER TIME

> **"** Learn to adjust yourself to the conditions you have to endure, but make a point of trying to alter or correct conditions so that they are most favorable to you. **"**
> —William Frederick Book

STEP 6: ADJUST THE PLAN OVER TIME

AT WORK

The caregiving phase of your life may last several weeks or stretch out over a number of years. Often, we don't know how long we will be involved in caregiving. The course of an older person's illness or disability can be unpredictable.

And the demands of your job will change over time. Special projects come and go. There are busy seasons and slack seasons in many industries. Therefore, you should expect to make some changes in your work schedule and arrangements.

Continue to write down changes in your work/life file. Use this information, along with feedback from your supervisor and co-workers, to change your plan, as needed. Keep these points in mind:

- Caregiving can be emotionally demanding and draining. It's important to seek out and listen to the opinions of others about how you are doing—and about whether or not your work/balance plan is working out. It's easy to become so caught up in caregiving demands that you lose objectivity about your work performance.

- Stick to the timeframes you set for yourself when you created your plan. If the plan called for an assessment after 30 or 60 days, conduct the assessment. Take a step back to look anew at your situation.

- Prepare a short, written summary of the trial period. Are things working out the way you thought they would? Share your summary with co-workers and ask for their feedback.

- After you have received input from co-workers, include their feedback in a written report to your supervisor.

- Needed changes may become obvious once you have honestly assessed your current situation. Be proactive. Incorporate proposed changes in your report.

- Request a meeting time to review your report with your supervisor.

- When you meet, talk about the work load and business goals of your department as well as your own needs and circumstances.

- Be open to compromise in creating changes to your plan.

- Set a timeframe for re-evaluating your work arrangement—and stick to it, again.

STEP 6: ADJUST THE PLAN OVER TIME

CAREGIVING

Expect the plan of care that you develop to change over time. Sometimes, small adjustments in the tasks performed by a home care aide or modifications to home surroundings can help the elder live independently for a longer period of time. In other circumstances, you may need to take decisive action. For example, if the behavior of a person with Alzheimer's disease threatens his or her safety or the safety of others, you may need to look into a new living arrangement.

If you have kept the elder and family members informed of the changes you are seeing in the elder's condition, then you will probably find that making needed changes to the plan of care will go smoothly. When major changes are indicated, like a move to another type of housing or facility, consider convening a family meeting to assure a common understanding of the facts and to air different views of the appropriate response.

Use the techniques and forms described in Step 1 to re-assess the situation and adjust the caregiving plan as needed.

PART 3

SPECIAL CONCERNS

LGBT CAREGIVERS

Nearly two-thirds of older adults who are lesbian, gay, bi-sexual, or transgender say they consider their friends to be chosen family, according to the Family Caregiving Alliance (FCA). Being a member of both a chosen family and a family of origin creates situations where an LGBT person may become a primary caregiver for a spouse, domestic partner, or legal spouse, a close friend who is also LGBT, or an aging parent or other relative—sometimes simultaneously. In the LGBT community—with older adults twice as likely to be single and living alone, and three to four times less likely to have children—a family of choice is depended upon to provide support and care.

Like others, LGBT caregivers face concerns about scheduling time off with their employer to care for an aging loved one. This concern may be further complicated by the degree to which you are "out" at work, and whether your employer has a nondiscrimination policy that affirms LGBT people and offers domestic-partner benefits. Ask your human resources department for written copies of your company's policies and benefits. Discuss any concerns with your manager or supervisor. FCA advises that, if you are not "out" to your employer or do not feel comfortable discussing personal issues with your manager or HR department, seek referrals for legal advice from local or nearby LGBT organizations, the *National Center for Lesbian Rights* (available to all LGBT people), http://www.nclrights.org/ or Lambda Legal https://www.lambdalegal.org.

Straight folks caring for LGBT elders face a separate set of challenges, for example: being supportive of the elder who may face discrimination and rejection by his or her peers and helping find senior housing that's accepting and welcoming.

Local LGBT community centers provide information, support, and advocacy for the rights of LGBT persons and their family members/caregivers. To find the center nearest you, visit https://www.lgbtcenters.org/LGBTCenters.

CHILDREN AND CAREGIVING

For millions of Americans, caregiving takes place within multi-generation families. Sometimes referred to as the Sandwich Generation, many middle-aged men and women are "sandwiched" between caring for an older relative and raising their own children.

Children are affected by your involvement in caregiving. As you stretch your time and energy to attend to their needs as well as those of the elder, conflicts will arise. And there will be opportunities for learning—about human caring, about family ties, about completing the cycle of life. The lessons your children learn by observing you and participating in caring for an aged relative will last a lifetime.

Children are full of thoughts and feelings about what is going on. They have a right, like everyone else in the family, to be:

- told the truth,
- given as much information as is appropriate for their age,
- invited to express their feelings without judgement, and
- involved in caregiving in ways in which they are comfortable.

Offer opportunities for children to be involved. Even very young children can help. Just being there to hold grandma's hand or telling her about the day's events can add a sparkle to her day.

Watch for warning signs that your child may not be coping well with the stresses of caregiving in your household:

- The appearance of new and strange fears, such as fear of the dark, or strangers, or being alone, of sleeping alone.
- Insistence on having mother or father nearby and refusing to go to favorite places.
- Significant change in emotions, such as crying, sleep disturbances with nightmares, irritability, or withdrawal from friends.
  Sudden changes in school performance.

If one or more of these warning signs is present:

- Spend time with the child or children and talk the issues through.
- Make use of children's books (see below) that deal with aging and caregiving issues. Use these as a springboard for conversation.
- Talk to teachers if your child is getting into trouble or doing poorly in school.

If issues and problem behaviors persist, ask your pediatrician to refer you to a pediatric psychologist or psychiatrist, or ask the school psychologist for help.

FOR MORE INFORMATION

Many local *United Way* organizations operate a *First Call for Help* information and referral line that can refer you to child care resources in your area. Dial 2-1-1. For more information on the range of resources available via the 211 line, visit: https://www.unitedway.org/our-impact/featured-programs/2-1-1.

Some employers offer an *Employee Assistance Program* (EAP) that provides confidential counseling services on family issues. Also, your employer may offer a child care resource and referral service that can help you find child care and refer to you to a qualified counselor. Contact the human resources department at your place of employment.

Doing Good Together is a non-profit organization with an intergenerational focus, providing tools to both families and organizations to help raise compassionate, engaged children. You will find activities, resources, and support for making empathy and "giving back" a natural part of life's early lessons. Visit: https://www.doinggoodtogether.org/bhf-book-lists/picture-books-about-aging.

SOME CHILDREN'S BOOKS ON AGING AND AGING FAMILIES

Borltzer, Eran. *What is God?* Toronto: Firefly Books, 1989.

Brodsky, Beverly. *The Story of Job.* New York: George Braziller, 1986.

Gellman, Marc, and Thomas Hartman. *Where does God live? Questions and Answers for Parents and Children.* New York: Triumph Books, 1991

Greenwald, Nancy. *Grandpa Forgot My Name.* Austin, MN: Newborn Books, 1997

Krasny Brown, Laurie and Brown, Mark. *When Dinosaurs Die: A Guide to Understanding Death.* Little, Brown & Co., 1996.

Munsch, Robert. *Love You Forever.* Willowdale, Ontario, Canada: Firefly Books, 1993.

LONG DISTANCE CAREGIVING

Today, millions of Americans face the challenge of arranging elder care on a long-distance basis. The good news is that, thanks to Internet resources and new services, you can stay involved more easily than in the past. Here are some specific ideas for managing elder care on a long-distance basis:

- Be realistic about what role you can effectively play. If you can drive to mom's house in 90 minutes, you are more likely to regularly see what's going on with your own eyes than if a visit involves a cross-country flight.

- You need to rely on others to be your eyes and ears, to watch for changes in the older person's condition and situation: another family member, a neighbor of the elder, or a friendly visitor from the elder's church. mosque, synagogue, or social service agency.

- Use the "800" numbers and websites listed in the Community Resources section of this guide to find and arrange services in the elder's community.

- If the elder is frail or forgetful, look into whether he or she is eligible for a publicly funded case management program (see page 44) or engage a private geriatric care manager (see page 44) to assess the situation and arrange services.

- Stay in regular telephone contact.

- If your employer offers an elder care resource and referral service (see page 39), call the counselor or visit the website for advice and help with finding resources.

- Make the most of in-person visits. Plan ahead by making a list of questions and concerns. If there are other family members involved, arrange time for a family meeting (see page 34). If you are considering housing options, schedule visits to the facilities in advance. Allow time to introduce yourself to friends or neighbors who stop in regularly. Ask them to call you with observations or concerns.

- Give the benefit of the doubt to relatives/friends who see the older person on a regular basis. Before making a snap judgment about what needs to be done, listen well to those who are closest to the elder's situation.

PART 4

ELDER CARE RESOURCES FROM A TO Z

ADULT DAY CENTERS

An adult day center is a program that can offer comprehensive services at a single location, ranging from a health assessment to recreation, meals, nursing, and therapies. Transportation is sometimes provided. Adult day care can offer a safe, stimulating environment for the older participant, as well as a welcome break from daily responsibilities for the family caregiver. Most adult day care facilities are open regular business hours, Monday through Friday, 9-5.

For more information:

Visit the website of the National Adult Day Services Association at https://www.nadsa.org.

AFFORDABLE CARE ACT

The Patient Protection and Affordable Care Act (ACA), signed into law in 2010, ushered in significant changes for health care in the U.S. Policies enacted through ACA have had implications at all levels of health care in America—from individual beneficiaries and physicians to multi-billion-dollar insurance companies and the country's largest health care funders, Medicare and Medicaid. In addition to providing health care to an estimated 20 million additional Americans (National Center for Health Statistics, 2017) who have gained insurance coverage through Medicaid expansion or ACA's insurance exchange Marketplace. the Act has also fostered significant health care system changes aimed at curbing cost growth and creating incentives for higher-quality care.

The ACA has benefited many family caregivers, especially those with lower incomes, by making access to health insurance possible for themselves. In addition, the ACA expanded options for home and community-based long term care services that directly benefit low income elders and younger persons with disabilities, as well as their caregivers.

To learn more about the ACA and its potential benefit to you as a family caregiver see "What Every Caregiver Needs to Know About Health Insurance":
https://www.care.com/homepay/what-every-caregiver-needs-to-know-about-health-insurance-1312171243.

To enroll in health insurance under the ACA, visit https://www.healthcare.gov.

BOOKS

- Benson, Herbert. *The Relaxation Response*. New York: Harper Torch, 1975.
- Green, Fboni, I. Reflections from the Soul. Omaha, NE: Green Publishing, 2017. Serves as compassionate compass to guide you on the journey as you seek to understand, express, heal, and reconcile your pain and loss of a loved one.
- Jacobs, Barry J. *The Emotional Survival Guide for Caregivers: Looking After Yourself and Your Family While Caring for An Aging Parent*. New York, NY: Guilford Press, 2006.
- Jampolsky, Gerald. *Love Is Letting Go of Fear*. Berkeley, CA: Celestial Arts, 1979.

- Kabat-Zin, Jon. *Wherever You Go, There You Are: Mindfulness Meditation in Everyday Life*. New York, NY: Hachette Books, 2005.

- Mace, Nancy and Rabbins, Peter. *The 36-Hour Day: A Family Guide to Caring for Someone with Alzheimer's Disease*. Baltimore, MD: Johns Hopkins University Press, 1981.

- Meyer, Maria M. and Derr, Paula, R.N. *The Comfort of Home: An Illustrated Step-By-Step Guide for Caregivers*. Portland, OR: Caretrust Publications LLC. Special editions available addressing the needs of caregivers for persons with Alzheimer's disease, Parkinson's disease, and other conditions. Visit http://www.comfortofhome.com.

CASE MANAGEMENT

A case manager or care coordinator, usually a nurse or social worker, conducts an assessment of the elder's condition, develops a plan of care, arranges for needed services, and makes visits to the older person on a regular basis to monitor for changes in condition. The goal is to coordinate the right combination of support services to enable the elder to live independently for as long as possible. An increasing number of communities offer case management services as part of programs designed to assist elders with multiple health problems and disabilities. Some healthcare systems provide care management as part of an approach to managing chronic conditions like congestive heart failure, chronic obstructive pulmonary disease (COPD), and others.

Eligibility for publicly-funded case management services is often restricted to persons with lower incomes. Private geriatric care managers (see page 44) offer this service on a fee-for-service basis.

FAMILY CAREGIVER EDUCATION AND SUPPORT

Over time, the stress of providing and arranging care for an older loved one, especially for an elder suffering from Alzheimer's disease or another form of dementia, can take a toll on the health of the family caregiver. There are supports available to help you cope, among them: adult day care (described above), respite care, and caregiver support groups.

Respite care services give caregivers with a break from caregiving responsibilities and may be provided in the home by volunteers or paid staff, or in a residential setting, such as assisted living facility that provides hotel-like services plus health and safety monitoring. Providers can arrange respite care for an afternoon, a weekend, or longer. Public funding for respite care is very limited.

Support groups offer another alternative. Many caregivers find that sharing experiences and ideas with others in similar situations helps in regaining perspective and learning new strategies.

In some States, Medicaid will pay eligible family members for the care they provide for low-income elders via CDPAP (Consumer Directed Personal Assistance Program) and CDPAS (Consumer Directed Personal Assistance Services). These programs allow care recipients to hire almost any caregiver they choose, including the family member who is currently providing care. For more information, visit https://www.payingforseniorcare.com/medicaid-waivers/home-care.html.

The National Family Caregiver Support Program, administered by Area Agencies on Aging, provides information, training, and services to caregivers. Contact the *Elder Care Locator* 1-(800)-677-1116 or visit https://eldercare.acl.gov/Public/Index.aspx.

ONLINE SUPPORT

Online resources to assist caregivers abound. These include chat rooms for caregivers, searchable databases of programs and services, tips on caregiving techniques and technologies, and other information.

Some good websites to start your search:

- *Caregiver Action Network* (CAN) is a non-profit consumer group dedicated to improving the lives of caregivers: https://caregiveraction.org or call (800)-896-3650.

- *National Alliance for Caregiving* (NAC) www.caregiving.org or call (301)-718-8444. The NAC website includes the Family Care Resource Connection, a comprehensive listing, with reviews of books, magazines, websites, and fact sheets related to family caregiving.

- *The Family Caregiver Alliance* (FCA) at www.caregiver.org or call (800)-445-8106. FCA offers online support groups for caregivers, and much more. (800)-445-8106.

- *Today's Caregiver* magazine provides insights and useful links at www.caregiver.com.

Also see the listing of Voluntary Health Organizations, beginning on page 100.

FINANCES—PAYING FOR CARE

LONG TERM CARE INSURANCE

Neither Medicare nor Medicare Supplemental Insurance nor private health insurance cover chronic conditions or long-term care. Private insurance companies offer long-term care insurance to fill this gap.

Long-term care (LTC) insurance can cover the cost of care in a nursing home or in the home and community. Such care may include the cost nursing, and physical therapy as well as personal care. LTC insurance can provide protection against financial losses and assure the policyholder a wider range of choices about the type of services he or she receives and where services are received. The older the consumer, the more likely that he or she may need long-term care assistance. Therefore, premiums for long-term care insurance increase with age. A portion of the premium paid for a tax-qualified LTC insurance policy may be tax deductible.

To make a good decision about whether long-term care insurance makes sense for you or for an older relative, you must weigh such policy features as elimination periods, inflation protection, and levels of care that are covered.

For more information:

- The AARP Webplace at www.aarp.org offers a primer on long-term care insurance features.

- Consumer Reports offers a guide to long-term care insurance policies
  https://www.consumerreports.org/long-term-care-insurance/long-term-care-insurance-gets-a-makeover

MEDICARE

Medicare is federal health insurance for persons over 65 and certain disabled people under age 65. Most people over 65 who have been employed or who are married to or divorced from someone who was employed are eligible for Medicare. The program is run by the Centers for Medicare and Medicaid (CMS), in cooperation with the Social Security Administration. Others may be eligible to enter the program by paying a premium or by meeting certain income limits. Medicare is divided into four parts: A, B, C, and D.

Part A is hospital insurance. Part B is medical insurance. Part A covers most hospital bills and a limited amount of home care, and nursing home care. Medicare beneficiaries are responsible for certain deductibles and co-payments. Most people do not pay a monthly Part A premium because they or a spouse has 40 or more quarters of Medicare-covered employment.

Part B covers medical bills, including most doctor's fees, medical equipment, diagnostic tests, outpatient care and some medications. A monthly premium is required and can be deducted automatically from Social Security payments. The annual deductible must be met before payments begin and a co-payment of 20% is required in most cases.

Medicare Part C includes Medicare Advantage Plans, like Health Maintenance Organizations (HMOs) and Preferred Provider Organizations (PPOs). These are managed care plans and other options offered by private insurance companies from which Medicare beneficiaries may choose. If you belong to a Medicare Advantage Plan that offers Medicare prescription drug coverage (see below), the monthly premium paid to the plan includes an amount for prescription drug coverage. Some plans charge no premium.

Medicare Part D provides options for prescription drug coverage for everyone with Medicare. This coverage may help lower prescription drug costs and help protect against higher costs in the future. If you join a Medicare drug plan, you usually pay a monthly premium. Part D is optional. If the beneficiary decides not to enroll in a Medicare drug plan when he or she first becomes eligible, the beneficiary may pay a penalty. These plans are run by insurance companies and other private companies approved by Medicare. Most Part D drug plans charge a premium that varies by plan. This is in addition to the Part B premium. Beneficiaries with limited income and resources may be eligible for extra help to pay for prescription drugs.

All the options are described in the *Medicare and You* handbook, issued annually by the *Centers for Medicare and Medicaid* (CMS).

For more information:

Contact the official Medicare website at www.Medicare.gov or call 1-(800)-MEDICARE (633-4227) and ask for a copy of the booklet *Medicare and You*. TTY users should call 1-(877)-486-2048.

Beneficiaries can enroll for MyMedicare.gov on the web where he or she can view claims, order forms and publications and more.

MEDICARE SUPPLEMENTAL INSURANCE

Commonly known as Medigap, Medicare supplemental insurance is commercially sold insurance that is tailored to provide gap-filling coverage for people on Medicare. Depending on the policy, Medigap policies pay some or all of Medicare deductibles and co-payments and may also pay for some health services not covered by Medicare, for example: coinsurance for doctor bills, hospital deductible, coinsurance for hospital expenses after a 60-day stay, or nursing home coinsurance after the Medicare coverage expires. The policies require, as does Medicare, that the services provided be medically necessary. Most policies will pay only up to the amount approved by Medicare.

For more information:

For free counseling and assistance with medical insurance matters, contact the *Senior Health Insurance Program* (SHIP), funded by the federal *Centers for Medicare and Medicaid*. For the telephone number for the SHIP program in your state, call the *Eldercare Locator* at 1-(800)-677-1116 or visit www.Medicare.gov.

MEDICAID

Financed with a combination of state and federal money, Medicaid is a program of medical assistance for low income persons who are 65 years of age or older, blind or disabled persons, and younger persons and their families who meet low-income eligibility standards. Medicaid is the largest public payment source for long term care.

Medicaid rules vary state-by-state. Older persons with limited income and assets may qualify for Medicaid coverage that includes payment for nursing facility services, home health care for those eligible for nursing facility services, and other services that vary from state-to-state. In general, a single individual may qualify for Medicaid if he or she owns no more than a home, personal belongings, a car and a small amount of savings. The standards vary. It may be possible for the beneficiary to protect some assets and still become eligible for Medicaid, but limitations apply and they vary from state to state and from year to year. Consult an attorney who specializes in elder law to assure prudent decision-making in relation to protecting assets and other Medicaid matters.

Under the Affordable Care Act (ACA), many states have expanded Medicaid options for home and community-based services with the goal of enabling frail elders and persons with disabilities. Programs vary from state-to-state. Your local Area Agency on Aging or state Medicaid office are good sources of information about the options available in your area.

For more information:

For information about Medicaid eligibility rules in each of the 50 states, visit call the *Elder Care Locator* 1-(800)-677-1116 for the telephone numbers of the SHIP health insurance counseling service in your state and the state Medicaid office.

Due to the complex and changing nature of Medicaid rules, you may wish to confer with an attorney specializing in elder law. The *National Academy of Elder Law Attorneys* publishes a booklet *How to*

Choose an Elder Law Attorney and offers a searchable database of its members on its website. Contact the Academy at (520)-881-4005 or www.naela.org.

MEDICAID—GETTING PAID TO BE A CAREGIVER FOR A FAMILY MEMBER

According to AARP, "All 50 states and the District of Columbia offer Medicaid waiver self-directed long-term services and supports (LTSS) programs that allow qualified individuals to manage their own care—meaning that people can hire and fire their own caregivers. Some states permit the care recipient to hire a family member to provide care.

- Eligibility, benefits, coverage and rules differ from state to state. Some programs pay family caregivers but exclude spouses and legal guardians. Others will pay care providers only if they do not live in the same house. Medicaid home care benefits also depend on the Medicaid program in which you are enrolled.

- Program names also vary. What is called Consumer Directed Care in one state is called Participant Directed Care in another. Among the many names: Self-Directed Care, In-Home Supportive Services, Cash, and Counseling.

- To qualify for Medicaid the recipient must not exceed the program's annual income and countable assets, not counting home value.

STEP BY STEP

Step 1: If your family member qualifies and is ready to join the more than 1 million people already participating in self-directed care plans, contact your state Medicaid office to begin the process.

Step 2: The applicant (with assistance, if desired or needed) is assessed for risks, needs, strengths, capacities, and preferences as required by Centers for Medicare & Medicaid Services.

Step 3: Your family member and any chosen representatives create a written service plan detailing the daily living assistance required—including bathing, dressing, moving from bed to wheelchair, light housekeeping, meal preparation, feeding, laundry, supervision, shopping, transportation, and medication compliance. There should be contingency plans for coverage when the care provider is off, and instructions on how fill-in caregivers should address risks.

If the assessment shows the need, a budget for goods and services will be provided.

Step 4: When the care plan is set, the participant (or surrogate, if needed) chooses a caregiver.

More information:

AARP article: "Can I get paid to be a caregiver for a family member?"
https://www.aarp.org/caregiving/financial-legal/info-2017/you-can-get-paid-as-a-family-caregiver.html.

MEDICAID—PROGRAM OF ALL-INCLUSIVE CARE FOR THE ELDERLY (PACE)

The PACE program provides comprehensive medical and social services to certain frail, elderly individuals living at home, most of whom are dually eligible for Medicare and Medicaid benefits. An interdisciplinary team of health professionals provides coordinated care that enables most participants to remain in the community rather than receive care in a nursing home. PACE becomes the sole source of Medicaid and Medicare benefits for participants. Financing for the program is capped, which allows providers to deliver all services participants need rather than limit them to those reimbursable under Medicare and Medicaid fee-for-service plans. To qualify, a person must be age 55 or older, live in the service area of a PACE organization, be eligible for nursing home care, and be able to live safely in the community.

For more information:

Visit www.medicaid.gov or contact the National PACE Association at https://www.npaonline.org or (703) 535-1565

REVERSE MORTGAGES

A reverse mortgage converts the equity in the home into cash without selling the home or having to make regular loan payments. The loan does not have to be repaid as long as the elder lives in the home. The money can be used for many different purposes, including purchasing home care services and making home modifications to improve safety and accessibility. Plan features vary from state to state.

For more information:

National Center for Home Equity Conversion: www.reverse.org or call the Center at (651)-222-6775.

AARP: https://www.aarp.org/money/credit-loans-debt/reverse_mortgages.

SUPPLEMENTAL SECURITY INCOME (SSI)

The Supplemental Security Income (SSI) program works in combination with Medicaid. Overseen by the Social Security Administration, SSI provides financial assistance, based upon need, to individuals who are aged (65+), blind, or disabled. To qualify for a monthly SSI benefit, a person's financial resources and income must fall below a specified level. In some states, persons who receive SSI are automatically eligible for Medicaid. To apply for SSI, contact your local Social Security office. For the number of the office nearest you, call (800)-772-1213 or visit https://secure.ssa.gov/ICON/main.jsp.

HOME CARE

COMPANIONSHIP—COMBATING ISOLATION

Living in isolation can be deadly. Companionship services, often arranged on a volunteer-basis by churches, social service agencies or home care providers, can assure regular social contact for an elder who lives alone. A visit by a companion can also provide a much-needed break for the family caregiver. Many faith-based organizations offer companions who will visit a disabled person at home.

Telephone reassurance services arrange for a volunteer to call and chat with the elder on a daily basis. Senior centers, hospitals, faith-based organizations, and social service agencies sponsor such programs.

The Village Movement—An Emerging Alternative for Social Connection

Membership organizations for persons who are 50 and older are springing up around the U.S. Beacon Hill Village in Boston was among the first of these groups. The Village to Village website describes the Village movement mission as "helping their members age in a place of their choosing, closely connected to their communities and with the supports and tools they need to create successful aging of their own design, providing social activities that minimize isolation and promote interaction and trust within the Village community, between individuals who offer their help and those who ask for help when needed."

For more information:

To find out if there is a faith-based volunteer companion program in your community, contact *Faith in Action*, a national volunteer movement that brings together religious congregations from many faiths and other community organizations. Call toll-free at (877)-324-8411 or visit www.fiavolunteers.org.

Village to Village website: https://www.vtvnetwork.org.

AARP guide: "How to Hire a Caregiver" at
https://bit.ly/2u1H3Ck.

HOME HEALTH CARE

Home health agencies can deliver a wide range of skilled medical care to patients in their own homes. Working together under the direction of a physician, a home health care team may include a visiting nurse, occupational, physical, or speech therapist, social worker, and home health aide. Today, seriously ill patients can receive high-tech care at home. Home health care includes assistive devices, like wheelchairs and walkers, as well as medical equipment like hospital beds, prostheses and oxygen. A home health agency will assess the patient's needs at home and arrange for the full spectrum of care.

Medicare pays for a limited amount of in-home care authorized by a doctor. To qualify, an individual must be homebound, require a skilled service like nursing or physical therapy, have a condition from which he or she is likely to recuperate, and need services on less than a full-time basis. To receive reimbursement under Medicare or Medicaid, a home health agency must be certified by Medicare and meet requirements overseen by the Department of Health in the state in which the agency provides service. Many states also require that home health agencies meet licensure requirements.

Home health care agencies may be public or private, for-profit or not-for-profit, and may be community based, like Visiting Nurse Associations, or hospital based. Continuing labor shortage problems have made it difficult to obtain needed home care services in many communities. Providing as much advance notice as possible to the home health agency can increase your chances of arranging the hours of care needed by your loved one.

For more information:

To find home health agencies in your community, contact your state Department of Health, which maintains a listing of certified home health agencies. For a copy of How to Choose A Home Care Agency: A Consumer Guide, contact the National Association for Home Care at (202)-547-7424 or visit https://www.nahc.org/consumers-information/home-care-hospice-basics/right-home-care-provider.

NON-MEDICAL HOME CARE SERVICES

Non-medical home care services, like homemaker or personal care services, can make all the difference for an elder who needs a little help to continue living independently at home. Such services may include the hands-on care of a home care aide or personal care attendant (who can help dress, bathe, and feed the elder) or assistance with daily tasks like cleaning, meal preparation, grocery shopping, or heavier household chores like cleaning an oven, fixing a broken window, or yard work. Home care agencies that provide these kinds of help are generally not Medicare-certified. Some states require home care agencies to be licensed or meet accreditation standards.

In some states, low-income elders may be eligible for home care services under Medicaid or state funded programs. Private agencies offer homemaker and other services on a fee-for-service basis. As with home health care, non-medical home care providers face serious labor shortages in many parts of the country. You and your family will benefit from doing as much advance planning as possible to arrange needed care. To find an agency, see the sources listed above, under Home Health Care.

For more information:

AARP guide: "How to Hire a Caregiver" at
https://bit.ly/2u1H3Ck.

HOSPICE CARE—A GOOD DEATH

Most Americans prefer to die at home, but less than a quarter actually do. The majority die in hospitals or nursing homes. And only about one-third of adults have an advance directive expressing their wishes for end-of-life care.

Advances in pain management techniques make it possible for most terminally ill patients to live out their final days in comfort. Simple-to use, legally-binding forms exist, making it possible for all of us to clearly express our wishes regarding whether or not to use medical technology to prolong life in dire medical circumstances. An increasing number of medical institutions offer palliative care for those with advanced terminal illnesses—a type of care that emphasizes pain control, symptom management, and personal care, instead of high-tech medical interventions in pursuit of an unattainable cure.

It is important to know your loved one's wishes before a crisis. Discuss these issues while the elder is able to communicate. See the Legal section, beginning on page 93, to review the types of important written documents that should be prepared.

HOSPICE CARE

Hospice care is a covered benefit under Medicare and Medicaid (in most states) and most private insurance plans. Hospice enables a person with a terminal illness to receive specialized care at home, in a nursing home or hospice residence, with the support of family, friends, and caring professionals. The emphasis is on pain control, comfort measures, and counseling to provide social, spiritual, physical and practical support for the dying patient and his or her family. Medical professionals oversee the delivery of hospice care. Over 90% of hospice care is provided in patients' homes.

Eligibility requirements for Medicare-certified hospice care include 1) a doctor's certification based on the natural history of the disease, that a patient is terminally ill (i.e., that the patient's life expectancy is six months or less, 2) the patient elects to receive care from a hospice program instead of standard Medicare benefits, 3) care is provided by a certified hospice program, and 4) the patient is eligible for Medicare Part A benefits. Medicare will pay for nursing services; doctor's services; drugs (including outpatient drugs for pain relief and symptom management); physical, occupational, and speech-language therapy; home health aides and homemaker services; medical social services; medical supplies and appliances; short-term inpatient care and inpatient respite care; training and interdisciplinary counseling for the patient and family members, and bereavement services for a full year after death.

For more information:

Consumer Reports Guide to Choosing Hospice Care.
https://www.consumerreports.org/hospice-care/choosing-hospice-care-guide.

Aging with Dignity, a non-profit organization, offers an easy-to-complete workbook for planning for care at the end of life, called Five Wishes, as well as its Next Step Guide that provides guidance on how to talk to loved ones about these issues. Contact *Aging with Dignity* at (888)-5-WISHES or www.agingwithdignity.org.

The Center for Practical Bioethics offers a free booklet called Caring Conversations. Call (800)-344-3829 or visit www.practicalbioethics.org.

HOUSING

Today, older persons can choose from a wider range of housing options than ever before. You can obtain information about the availability of the full range of local housing options by contacting the Area Agency on Aging (AAA) serving the community in which the elder lives. Call or visit the *Elder Care Locator* at (800)-677-1116 www.eldercare.gov.

ACCESSORY APARTMENTS

An accessory apartment is a home within a home—a living unit created for the purpose of allowing an older relative to live in his or her own quarters, with family nearby to provide or arrange support care, as needed. Check to see if local zoning regulations allow accessory apartments. Benefits of accessory apartments include privacy for the elder, less travel and wear-and-tear for caregivers, and continued contact among multiple generations.

For more information:

Visit *AARP* at https://bit.ly/2UsVMSL.

AFFINITY RETIREMENT COMMUNITIES

A traditional retirement community is an age-restricted, usually 55+ community that enables older adults to live independently but with access to social activities and community amenities, such as yard maintenance services or fitness and recreation facilities. (Retirement destinations such as Florida and Arizona have many such places.)

A "niche" or "affinity" retirement community is one where residents share a common interest, religion or identity. The link may revolve around, for example, shared ethnicity, sexual orientation, occupation, hobby.

For more information:

See the *AARP* Livable Communities—Six Creative Housing Options:
https://www.aarp.org/livable-communities/info-2014/creative-age-friendly-housing-options.html.

ASSISTED LIVING

Assisted living is a combination of housing and supportive services including personal care (such as bathing and dressing) and household management (such as meals and housekeeping) that stresses privacy, dignity, autonomy, and individuality. The goal is to provide the resident help only as needed. Residences vary in size and style, from apartment or hotel-style structures to smaller, family-style homes. Some assisted living residences have secure units or wings designed to serve persons with Alzheimer's disease and other forms of dementia.

The definition of Assisted Living varies from state to state, as do regulations. Assisted living is designed for persons don't need the medical oversight and 24-hour nursing care provided in a nursing home. Assisted living may be the right choice for an elder who:

- needs some help with activities like housekeeping, meals, bathing, dressing, or medication reminders,
- would like the socialization benefits and the security of having assistance available on a 24-hour basis in a residential environment.

Assisted living is usually paid for privately. Some States include coverage under Medicaid. Costs can range from $2,400 to over $5,000 per month. Benefits can include increased socialization, better nutrition, supervision of medications, and the ability to add services as they are required.

For more information:

Consumer Reports provides a guide to choosing the right assisted living option at https://www.consumerreports.org/elder-care/choosing-the-right-assisted-living-community.

Most states regulate assisted living and publish consumer guides specific to the state. Call or visit *Eldercare Locator* (800)-677-1116 https://eldercare.acl.gov/Public/Index.aspx and contact your State Unit on Aging.

Leading Age (see consumer information tab) https://www.leadingage.org.

CONGREGATE HOUSING

Like Assisted Living, congregate housing offers a combination of housing and services for elders who have some limitations in ability to perform everyday tasks or who want social interaction. Generally consisting of individual apartments with areas for group socializing and dining, congregate housing caters to people who are fairly self-sufficient, mobile, and require no special care. Congregate housing built with federal, state, and local funds will have income eligibility requirements. Licensure varies state-by-state. For a list of facilities in your state, call or visit *Eldercare Locator* (800)-677-1116 https://eldercare.acl.gov/Public/Index.aspx and contact your State Unit on Aging.

CONTINUING CARE RETIREMENT COMMUNITIES

A Continuing Care Retirement Community (CCRC) combines housing, personal care, and skilled nursing care on a single campus. CCRC's offer an environment and the services necessary for residents to "age in place." This means that, as personal and health care needs change, the elder can remain living in the same community.

Entering a CCRC usually involves a substantial one-time entrance fee, plus a monthly fee. In order for the CCRC to deliver contracted services over a long period of time, it must be financially sound. Not all states assure the financial stability of CCRC developers and managers. Before signing a CCRC contract, review the contract in detail, especially the CCRC's financial statements, with particular attention to whether or not the CCRC has sufficient reserves to remain solvent over time.

For more information:

For information on CCRC's in your state, call or visit *Eldercare Locator* (800)-677-1116 https://eldercare.acl.gov/Public/Index.aspx and contact your State Unit on Aging.

See the *AARP* article "About Continuing Care Retirement Communities" at https://www.aarp.org/caregiving/basics/info-2017/continuing-care-retirement-communities.html.

ECHO HOUSING

Sometimes called a "granny flat" or an in-law apartment, an Elder Cottage Housing Opportunity (ECHO) unit is a small, manufactured home that can be installed in the back or on the side of a single-family residence and removed when it is no longer needed. It is designed specifically for frail older persons or persons with disabilities and is intended to enable them to live near family and friends who will provide the support necessary for them to live independently. The addition of an ECHO unit to an existing home or property is contingent on local zoning regulations.

MEDCottage is a form of ECHO housing—a mobile, modular medical dwelling designed to be temporarily placed on a caregiver's property for rehabilitation and extended care. According the MEDCottage website http://www.medcottage.com/home.html: "It's a state-of-the-art hospital room with remote monitoring available so caregivers and family members have peace of mind knowing they are providing the best possible care."

For more information:

https://homeguides.sfgate.com/inlaw-apartment-45307.html.

HOME MODIFICATIONS—STAYING AT HOME

Most older people want to continue to live in their own homes for as long as possible. Most family members want to help them do this as well, but they often have concerns about the older person's safety and security. Today, through a combination of home modifications and in-home personal services, many frail elders can live at home longer than ever before.

Home modifications are changes that you can make to the living environment to increase ease of use, safety, security, and independence. Examples of home modifications include: wheelchair lifts; automated chairs to go up and down stairs; lever door handles that operate easily with a push; handrails on both sides of staircase and outside steps; ramps for accessible entry and exit; walk-in showers; grab bars by the toilet, in the shower, and by the tub; and sliding shelves and lazy susans in corner cabinets.

Many home modification materials are available from home repair retailers and medical equipment companies. In some areas, private companies specializing in home modification can assess the home and make needed changes.

For more information:

Visit the website of the *National Resource Center on Supportive Housing and Home Modification* at www. homemods.org, or call the Center at (213)-740-1364.

HOME SHARING

Home sharing is an option that may make sense for an older person who wishes to continue to live in his or her own home but who needs someone else to help share expenses and upkeep. A program coordinator interviews homeowners and older or younger individuals to determine suitability and to make matches that may be long or short in duration. Home sharing arrangements can address the elder's need for rental income, companionship, and performance of household chores, like light cleaning and yard work.

For more information: *The National Home Sharing Resource Center* https://nationalsharedhousing.org describes home sharing options and includes a national directory of programs.

LIVING TOGETHER IN YOUR HOME

In a crisis situation, like a sudden hospitalization of one of your parents, you may instinctively think of inviting an older loved to come live in your home. It is wise to carefully consider such a move. Take into account the views and feelings of all family members involved, including children if you have any.

Ask yourself these questions:

- Is your home equipped for this? Most importantly, do you have enough space in the right location? If you live in a larger home, are there separate living quarters (private bath, separate bedroom) in an accessible location? Upstairs won't work if the elder is becoming frailer.

- How well do you get along? Is your personality and the personalities of your spouse or significant other compatible with the elder? If it's been a rocky emotional road up until now, it is not likely to smooth out when the older person moves in.

- How do other members of the family feel? What's the history of the relationship between your spouse (if you have one) and each of your children with the elder? Hold a family meeting (see page 34) before taking any action. Will your desire to care for mom or dad disrupt relationships within the rest of your household?

- How much care and attention does the elder need now—and how much will be needed in the foreseeable future?

If you decide to have the older person move in with you, set a trial period of two months or so, during which the older person continues to maintain his or her own home or apartment.

If you haven't settled into a compatible relationship by the end of the trial period, consider another housing arrangement. Don't wait until you are physically or emotionally exhausted or tensions are running at an all-time high. You owe it to yourself, the elder, and the rest of your family to make a change before strains result in damaged relationships.

THE SMART HOME

Smart homes, which incorporate environmental and wearable medical sensors, actuators, and modern communication and information technologies, can enable continuous and remote monitoring of elders' health and wellbeing. Smart homes may allow an older person to stay in a comfortable home environment instead of moving to a more expensive healthcare facility that limits independence. Healthcare personnel can also keep track of the overall health condition of the elderly in real-time and provide feedback and support from distant facilities.

For more information:

National Institute on Aging: Guide to Best Technology Resources and Tools for Seniors: https://www.ioaging.org/the-2018-guide-to-best-technology-resources-and-tools-for-seniors.

SUBSIDIZED HOUSING

So-called "senior housing" developments offer an affordable housing alternative for many older Americans because rents are based on the elder's income and subsidized by federal, state, or local programs. Therefore, elders must meet income and asset eligibility guidelines. A typical senior housing development offers one-bedroom units with a separate kitchen and bath and usually includes a common room for social activities such as arts and crafts, recreation, or meals programs. If you feel this could be an attractive alternative, plan ahead. Waiting lists of several years are not uncommon in some areas.

The housing choice voucher program is the federal government's major program for assisting very low income families, the elderly, and the disabled to afford decent, safe, and sanitary housing in the private market.

For more information:

Contact your local Area Agency on Aging via the *Eldercare Locator* (800)-677-1116 https://eldercare.acl.gov/Public/Index.aspx.

Housing Choices Vouchers Fact Sheet at U.S. Department of Housing and Urban Development https://www.hud.gov/topics/housing_choice_voucher_program_section_8.

LEGAL

Depending on the physical and mental health of the elder, there are a number of decisions related to finances, healthcare, and what is to be done after death that require legal advice and legal documents.

Most importantly, elders and their families must communicate with each other before a crisis arises so that, in the event that the elder dies or is incapacitated, there is clarity about who is legally authorized to handle the elder's affairs—and what the elder's wishes are.

Family caregivers should be sure to have in place legal documents important to the lifelong care of the elder. These include a Durable Power of Attorney (DPOA), a Health Care Proxy, and—depending on the elder's wishes—a Do Not Resuscitate (DNR) order.

These documents are particularly important because if there is no DPOA or Health Care Proxy, and it develops that the elder lacks capacity to make financial or health decisions, then a Guardianship (over the person) or Conservatorship (over finances only) may need to be established by a court proceeding. This can be an expensive and complex legal process at a time when the elder and family face a medical situation or crisis.

The following information provides an introduction to the documents that you should have available. This information is not intended to substitute for legal advice.

DURABLE POWER OF ATTORNEY

Durable Power of Attorney is a document that grants a person or persons (called "Attorney-in-fact") the legal powers to perform on behalf of the elder "Grantor" certain acts and functions specifically outlined in the document. This power is effective immediately and continues to be effective even if the Grantor becomes disabled or incompetent. The powers usually granted can include real estate, banking and financial transactions, personal and family maintenance, government benefits, real estate trust, and beneficiary transactions.

HEALTH CARE PROXY

A **Health Care Proxy** is a legal document that allows you to name a person (called a health care agent or proxy) to make health care decisions for you in the event that you are not able to do so for yourself. This document takes effect only if your physician determines in writing that you lack the capacity to make or communicate health care decisions. Any competent adult (18 or older) may serve as a health care agent, except the operator, administrator, or employee of a facility where you are a patient at the time you complete the health care proxy form—unless that person is related to you by blood, marriage or adoption. Acting with your authority, your agent or proxy can make any health care decision that you could, if you were able, and has the legal right to get any information, including confidential medical information, necessary to make informed decisions for you.

LIVING WILL

A type of advance directive, a **Living Will** is a written statement detailing a person's desires regarding their medical treatment in circumstances in which they are no longer able to express informed consent. Some states do not recognize a Living Will as binding on medical personnel.

For more information:

To find an attorney specializing in elder law, see the directory of the National Academy of Elder Law Attorneys at https://www.naela.org.

Visit the U.S. National Library of Medicine for an overview of advance directives, including living wills: https://medlineplus.gov/advancedirectives.html.

See the National Institute on Aging guide to Health Care Proxies and other advance care directives at https://www.nia.nih.gov/health/caregiving/advance-care-planning.

DO NOT RESUSCITATE (DNR) ORDER

A do-not-resuscitate order, or **DNR order**, is a medical order written by a doctor. It instructs health care providers not to do cardiopulmonary resuscitation (CPR) if a patient's breathing stops or if the patient's heart stops beating. If an elder does not want to have (CPR), a valid DNR order should be prepared and made part of his/her medical record. It is also essential to keep a DNR Order Verification form with the person at all times. A type of advance directive, this form verifies that there is a valid DNR order in the person's medical record and allows medical personnel, such as EMT's and paramedics, to provide care and transport in the community without defibrillation and intubation. The form is available at doctor's offices, hospitals and nursing homes and is signed by a doctor/nurse practitioner or physician assistant and by the individual or health care agent or representative.

VIAL OF LIFE

The Vial of Life Project http://www.vialoflife.com/vial-is-free/ provides an easy-to-complete form to document your healthcare wishes in an emergency situation. Upon completing the form, you receive a Vial of Life decal that you stick on your front door alerting paramedics where to find your medical information.

ESTATE PLANNING—WILLS AND TRUSTS

It is important that elders have the documents necessary to carry out their wishes after death. These include a properly drafted and up to date Will, and also, depending on the circumstances, Trusts that accomplish desired financial, estate, and legacy control and distribution. Even with estates that have no great complication, it is wise to have the help of an attorney in preparing these documents to be sure that they accomplish what the elder intends.

LEGAL PLANNING RESOURCES

Finding a lawyer who specializes in legal planning for elders is an important first step in evaluating legal needs. The *National Academy of Elder Law Attorneys* website offers a guide to help prepare for discussing your needs. Go to https://www.naela.org *Questions & Answers When Looking for an Elder Law Attorney*, or call (703)-942-5711 to request a copy.

FINDING SUBSIDIZED LEGAL SERVICES

Contact your local *Area Agency on Aging* (AAA) to obtain contact information on free or subsidized legal help available in your community. To find your local AAA, call the *Elder Care Locator* at (800)-677-1116. Or visit the Legal Service Corporation website to search its national directory of legal services programs https://www.lsc.gov/what-legal-aid/find-legal-aid.

MENTAL HEALTH SERVICES

If your older loved one shows on-going signs of confusion or depression (withdrawal from social relationships, apathy, crying, expression of feelings of hopelessness, changes in weight or sleep patterns), he or she may benefit from counseling or psychiatric support. About 20% of older adults have experienced some type of mental health concern—about one-third of them have not received treatment. Support groups for widows or widowers, often sponsored by senior centers, hospices, or faith-based groups, can ease the stress of life transitions and losses.

For more information:

Your local *Area Agency on Aging* may maintain a list of mental health providers that specialize in care of the elderly. Contact the national *Elder Care Locator*: (800)-677-1116 www.eldercare.gov.

Centers for Disease Control and Prevention: Article "Depression is not a normal part of growing older." https://www.cdc.gov/aging/mentalhealth/depression.htm Contains links to resources.

National Council on Aging, My Medicare Matters: Article: "Mental illness is not a "normal" part of aging." https://www.mymedicarematters.org/2017/05/mental-illness-is-not-a-normal-part-of-aging.

The local chapter of the *Alzheimer's Association* can provide referrals to resources for elders and families affected by Alzheimer's disease and other forms of dementia. Call (800)-272-3900 or visit www.alz.org.

NURSING HOMES

Today, the nursing home, also known as a skilled nursing facility, extended care facility, convalescent home, or rehab/continuing care facility, serves the needs of two specific groups of people: 1) those who need short-term, skilled care in a medical setting to recuperate, usually following a hospitalization, and 2) chronically ill persons who need on-going medical supervision and nursing assistance on a 24-hour a day basis. Services include nursing, personal care by certified nursing assistants, on-call physician services, meals, laundry services, counseling, recreation, nutrition counseling, social services, rehabilitation services, and laboratory and pharmacy services.

Average annual charges for nursing home care are $82,000-$93,000. Medicare pays for virtually no long-term nursing home care. Medicaid pays for nursing home care, but the elder must have limited financial means and the choice of nursing home will be restricted to those homes that accept Medicaid patients. See the section on Medicaid (see page 82) for more information about applying for Medicaid coverage.

WHEN IS NURSING HOME CARE THE RIGHT OPTION?

If you answer "yes" to these questions, nursing home care may be the right option:

- Does the older person need more care—especially medically related care—than it is practical to provide at home?

- Is the primary family caregiver feeling overwhelmed, physically or emotionally, with the demands related to care being provided at home?

- Is the older person behaving in ways that would make it impractical to live in another type of residential setting (e.g., dangerous wandering, incontinence, verbally or physically abusive)?

Many family members dread the thought of ever having to consider nursing home care for an older loved one. The image of the nursing home resident wasting away in a cold, impersonal institutional environment that smells of urine, receiving little personal care or attention, lingers. Such conditions do still exist in some nursing homes today, but they are far less common than in the past. In recent years, consumer advocates and government regulators have forced nursing homes to rethink their missions and the way they deliver care. In particular, many have cut back on the use of physical restraints and on the use of sedative medications as a way of controlling behavior of residents.

With proper research and a commitment to maintaining contact with the older person, you can arrange for nursing home care that assures safety and proper care for the older person while making it possible for family members to maintain a caring relationship with the elder.

CHOOSING A NURSING HOME

Any decision to consider nursing home care must be discussed with the older person, to the extent that he or she is mentally able to participate in the decision. Postponing such discussions only increases feelings of guilt and anxiety on the part of family members involved in the move. It dishonors the older person who is entitled, as matter of basic respect, to be kept informed of plans to make this type of significant life change.

Elder care professionals report that quality of life of the elder is often diminished when the elder and family wait too long before making a move to a facility that can provide a more intensive level of care. If you are the primary caregiver, you will need to take decisive action to assure that the elder obtains the level of care needed as health conditions change.

Nursing homes offer several levels of care, depending on the elder's medical condition and need for skilled and custodial care. Before researching specific nursing homes, consult with the older person's physician to determine what level of care is needed.

Good sources of recommendations about specific homes include the older person's physician, hospital social workers and clergy in the community. Ask which nursing homes have reputations for providing good quality care.

Visit several homes and take notes—not just about what you are told by staff of the nursing home, but about what you see, smell, and feel. Try to talk to other people who have family members in each facility of interest to you. See the information sources listed below to obtain checklists to use when making visits.

For more information:

The *National Consumer Voice for Quality Long Term Care* offers consumer information.

Visit https://theconsumervoice.org/home or call (202)-332-2275.

Every *State Office on Aging* operates a *Nursing Home Ombudsman Program* that provides information on nursing home residents' rights and investigates complaints. Contact the national *Elder Care Locator:* (800) 677-1116 www.eldercare.gov.

AARP: Article: "When it's time for a nursing home." https://www.aarp.org/caregiving/basics/info-2017/parents-nursing-home-choices-bjj.html.

Centers for Medicare and Medicaid Services (CMS) Medicare Compare program provides consumers with access to data to make an informed choice when shopping for nursing home care. Visit https://data.medicare.gov/data/nursing-home-compare.

NUTRITION

Good nutrition is essential to good health at any age. Older people, especially those who live alone, may not be motivated to shop for food or cook for themselves. Home delivered meals, Eating Together programs, and grocery delivery services are among the nutrition services that have been developed to help assure good nutrition for older people.

EATING TOGETHER

Senior centers and other community groups sponsor noontime meals for groups of seniors. Recreational, educational, or health-related activities are often organized before or after the meal. Transportation may be provided. Fees range from a small donation to a few dollars per meal. To find a local program, contact *Elder Care Locator*: (800)-677-1116 or visit www.eldercare.gov.

SUPPLEMENTAL NUTRITION ASSISTANCE PROGRAM (SNAP)

SNAP helps low-income households buy the food they need for a nutritionally adequate diet, offering nutrition assistance to millions of eligible, low-income individuals and families. SNAP is the largest program in the domestic hunger safety net.

Visit: https://www.fns.usda.gov/snap/supplemental-nutrition-assistance-program-snap.

GROCERY DELIVERY

An increasing number of supermarkets and social service agencies will arrange for delivery of a list of groceries to the elder's home. Cost varies depending on the vendor of the service.

HOME DELIVERED MEALS

Sometimes called "Meals on Wheels," home delivered meals help elders who are homebound or cannot prepare their own meals. Home delivered meals programs can usually accommodate special diet needs if informed in advance. Churches, senior centers, hospitals, and other community organizations sponsor these programs. Fees range from a minimal donation to a charge on a sliding scale related to the elder's income. To find a program in your area, contact the national *Elder Care Locator*: (800)-677-1116 or visit www.eldercare.gov.

PERSONAL EMERGENCY RESPONSE SYSTEMS

A personal emergency response—or medical alert—system can help provide the peace of mind if you are concerned about an elder who lives alone and may be at risk of falling or other emergencies. Most systems are offered by private companies. The elder wears a small pendant or wristband with a transmitter. If the elder falls or needs assistance, the system contacts a call center. If the older person does not answer a phone call from the call center responder, the responder dispatches help to the elder's home. More advanced systems may include fall-detection, dispensing of medications, and more.

More information:

Consumer Reports: Article: "How to choose a medical alert system."
https://www.consumerreports.org/medical-alert-systems/how-to-choose-a-medical-alert-system.

TELE-MEDICINE

New technological devices allow the physician or home health nurse to remotely monitor critical factors such as vital signs and medication compliance. Geriatric psychiatrists conduct therapy sessions remotely. The benefits of telemedicine can include increasing patient engagement, satisfaction, and convenience, providing remote and rural patients with access to care, and improving leverage of limited physician resources.

To find out which tele-medicine systems are available in your area, inquire with your physician, local hospital or home health agency.

For more information:

AARP article: "Using Telehealth to Improve Home-Based Care for Older Adults and Family Caregivers."
https://www.aarp.org/content/dam/aarp/ppi/2018/03/using-telehealth-to-improve-home-based-care-for-older-adults-and-family-caregivers.pdf.

TRANSPORTATION

A variety of community organizations and local transit systems offer rides to senior centers, shopping centers, and medical or other appointments. Some programs offer wheelchair-accessible vehicles. Generally, rides are free or a minimal fee is charged. Often, the elder must book a ride to a specific appointment well in advance. Contact the local *Area Agency on Aging* or senior center. To find a program in your area, contact the national *Elder Care Locator:* (800)-677-1116 or visit www.eldercare.gov.

VOLUNTARY HEALTH ORGANIZATIONS

The following organizations can provide valuable information and resources—both for persons with particular health conditions and for their caregivers:

- Alzheimer's Association, (800)-272-3900; www.alz.org
- American Autoimmune Related Diseases Association, (800)-598-4668; https://www.aarda.org
- American Cancer Society, (800)-227-2345; www.cancer.org
- American Diabetes Association, (800)-342-2383; www.diabetes.org
- American Foundation for AIDS Research (amfAR), (800)-392-6327; www.amfar.org
- American Heart Association, (800) 242-8721; https://www.heart.org/en/about-us
- American Kidney Fund, (800)-638-8299; www.kidneyfund.org
- American Liver Foundation, (800)-465-4837; www.liverfoundation.org
- American Lung Association® To connect to local offices (800)-LUNG-USA; www.lungusa.org
- American Parkinson Disease Association, (800)-223-2732; www.apdaparkinson.org
- American Stroke Association, (800) STROKES; www.stroke.org
- American Tinnitus Association, (800) 634-8978; www.ata.org
- Amyotrophic Lateral Sclerosis (ALS) Association, (800)-782-4747; www.alsa.org
- Arthritis Foundation (800) 283-7800; www.arthritis.org
- Asthma & Allergy Foundation of America, (800)-727-8462; www.aafa.org
- Cancer Research Foundation of America, (800)-227-CRFA; www.preventcancer.org
- Crohn's & Colitis Foundation of America, (800)-343-3637; www.ccfa.org
- Easter Seals Society, (800)-221-6827; www.easter-seals.org
- Epilepsy Foundation, (800)-EFA-1000; www.epilepsyfoundation.org
- The Foundation Fighting Blindness, (888)-394-3937, TDD: (800)-683-5551; www.blindness.org
- Huntington's Disease Society of America, (800)-345-HDSA; www.hdsa.org
- Kidney Cancer Association, (800) 850-9132; www.kidneycancerassociation.org
- The National Brain Tumor Society, (617) 924-9997; www.tbts.org
- The Leukemia & Lymphoma Society, (800) 955-4572; www.leukemia-lymphoma.org
- Lupus Foundation of America, (800) 558-0121; www.lupus.org
- Mental Health America (800)-969-NMHA (6642), TTY: (800)-433-5959 www.nmha.org
- Myasthenia Gravis Foundation of America, (800)-541-5454; www.myasthenia.org
- Myositis Association of America, (800)-821-7356; www.myositis.org
- National Alliance for the Mentally Ill, (800)-950-NAMI (6264); www.nami.org
- National Down Syndrome Society, (800)-221-4602; www.ndss.org

- National Hemophilia Foundation, (800)-42-HANDI; www.hemophilia.org
- National Multiple Sclerosis Society, (800)-FIGHT-MS; www.nationalmssociety.org
- National Osteoporosis Foundation, (202)-223-2226; www.nof.org
- National Psoriasis Foundation, (800)-723-9166; www.psoriasis.org
- National Sleep Foundation, www.sleepfoundation.org
- Osteogenesis Imperfecta Foundation, (844)-889-7579; www.oif.org
- The Paget Foundation, (212)-509-5335; https://www.iofbonehealth.org/national-societies/1284
- Sjogren's Syndrome Foundation, (800)-475-6473; https://www.sjogrens.org
- Spina Bifida Association of America, (800)-621-3141; http://spinabifidaassociation.org
- Tourette Association of America, (888)-486-8738; www.tsa-usa.org
- Tuberous Sclerosis Alliance, (800)-225-6872; www.tsalliance.org
- United Ostomy Association, (800)-826-0826; www.uoa.org
- U.S. Pain Foundation, (800)-910-2462; https://uspainfoundation.org

LIST OF FORMS

THOUGHTS FOR THE CAREGIVING JOURNEY

Your involvement in caring for an older person opens up opportunities for you to learn more about yourself—your levels of patience, stamina, and compassion, and your ability to listen well. Elder care also offers an opportunity to re-connect with an elder or to establish a new, positive rapport, walking with the elder on his or her unique aging journey. The potential positive benefits of caregiving can include feelings of love and self-satisfaction that accompany giving of yourself to another.

On the other hand, the elder may reject your attempts to arrange or provide care as unnecessary or unwanted. Such rejection of your assistance can open up old hurts and resentments.

What is important is the attitude you bring to the caregiving experience. The opportunity to provide elder care usually comes once in a lifetime. Whether your help is accepted or rejected, you will want to look back on this phase of life with the sense of peace that comes from knowing that you have done the best you could do in your own life situation.

Your ability to balance responsibilities at work and within your family will affect the quality of your elder caring experience. We hope that the principles, information and techniques described in this guide will contribute to a positive caregiving experience.

We invite your comments and suggestions so that future readers of this guide may learn from your experience.

Visit us at www.caregiverswork.com. Caregivers Work LLC is a community of professionals and family caregivers who share wisdom and expertise—and promote caregiver-friendly workplaces.

> " The story of life is quicker than
> the wink of an eye.
> The story of love is hello and goodbye.
> Until we meet again... "
> —Jimi Hendrix

NOTES

_____
_____
_____
_____
_____
_____
_____
_____
_____
_____
_____
_____
_____
_____
_____
_____
_____
_____
_____
_____
_____
_____
_____

Made in the USA
Columbia, SC
08 May 2019